TABLE OF CONTENTS

PREFACE

This is a book about equity and excellence. It is about more than that of course, but when I think of Avis Glaze, those are the first two words that always spring to mind. Maybe it's because she says these words often when she talks about how best to deliver quality education to students and teachers. More probably it's because she lives it. Whatever she does, she does with distinction. Along the way, she never fails to ask if what she is doing is fair and equitable. That is who Avis Glaze is, and the countless students and teachers who have encountered her influence along the way are all the better for it.

As someone who was privileged to work with Avis during her time as Chief Student Achievement Officer of Ontario and the founding CEO of the Literacy and Numeracy Secretariat, I knew early on that I wanted to write this book. This is not a biography focused on the personal, although we certainly learn some wonderful anecdotes during her life arc from Jamaica to Canada. It is a professionally focused biography that outlines most of her key innovations and initiatives, which she spearheaded over a long and successful career. The writing does not simply describe the initiative itself, but often how she made it happen in the first place. From this standpoint, then, it serves as a guide to others for what effective leadership in education looks like. That's what will hopefully make this book so valuable to teachers, principals, superintendents of education, elected education officials, policy makers, and anyone with a stake in education and leadership.

One section even includes some of the articles and thoughts from Avis herself on such key issues as leadership, literacy, and character development, while an extended Q & A section is a free-ranging conversation with her that gets to the heart of key issues. Topics as far reaching as poverty in education, how to deal with hate, the future role of the educator, nation building, and how she sees her own personal legacy are just some of the areas of emphasis. That makes this book an interesting blend of biography and conversation, a guide for educational excellence, and collection of essays for reflection and action.

If there is another phrase that defines Avis' philosophy and modus operandi, it is surely the subtitle of this book — "The Children Cannot Wait." As governments in Canada and around the world continue to debate and strategize about what to do to improve education — all with good intentions — the clock continues to tick louder and faster. Avis believes that now — not next year — is the time to refine our improvement agenda and redouble our efforts to enhance the life chances of the students we serve.

This book is a clarion call to educators at an opportune time in the history of education reform. Avis herself calls it the "Golden Age" of education. She feels that we now know what works in education. The evidence exists in many schools and districts. Educators worldwide who read this book will identify with an educator who taught at all levels in multiple settings. They will see their experiences, frustrations, and challenges, but more importantly their positive vision of what is still possible in education. They will walk away concluding that they must savour their successes, yet cannot rest on their laurels — because the children cannot wait.

–Roderick Benns

Avis Glaze
The Children Cannot Wait

Part One:
Origins and Early Days

CHAPTER ONE
"OUT OF MANY, ONE PEOPLE"

Jamaica is striking as a result of the spine of mountains that runs through its centre, east to west. From this central backbone, other mountain ranges run north and south, creating fingers of crests, hills, and valleys that define the nation's landscape. The Parish of Westmoreland, the most westerly region of the island nation, was founded in 1703 and is steeped in history. It's the place where Christopher Columbus once stopped on his second voyage to the Caribbean nation, and where pirate Henry Morgan set sail from Bluefields in 1670 for his raid on Panama City.

For Avis Glaze, it was also where her journey began, and where she first absorbed the high standards her parents expected of her. Her parents defined success for her and her four siblings in two ways — academic excellence, and becoming a good person with impeccable character and values. Character development, in fact, began at the dinner table. In a nation known for its powerful matriarchal influences, her mother was a strong figure within the family unit — and for Avis, personally. She instilled in Avis key lessons about treating all people with respect, no matter social class, abilities, race, or language. Avis remembers their gardener, a man named Bishop, who moved very slowly in everything he did, because of illness. At first, Avis used to watch him warily, as children do, wondering why he was different from other people. Her mother explained that he had a hernia and that she needed to be patient with him.

"We must never look down on others," her mother told her, no matter the differences.

Her mother also taught her lessons in generosity, forgiveness, kindness, respect, and most importantly to Avis, empathy.

This early inculcation of values would now — and certainly later in her life — help to shape many of her beliefs about leadership and how people should be treated.

She now looks back with amusement at an incident involving her grandmother, who lived with the family, as many grandparents do in Jamaica. She recalls her mother asking her grandmother if she had had her lunch. Her grandmother said no, she hadn't eaten anything all morning, even though Avis had witnessed her grandmother eat lunch just a short time before her mother arrived.

"I remember thinking, why is she lying?" Avis recalls, her sense of right and wrong sharply activated. "This really bothered me — the idea that my grandmother would lie to my mother."

However, in later years, Avis more fully understood that her grandmother suffered from Alzheimer's disease and simply hadn't remembered that she had eaten lunch.

Avis' family decided to move one parish eastward to St. Elizabeth on the southwestern coast where Avis would continue her zeal for education. Her desire to help others — to connect through learning and leading — grew stronger.

The Hills Beckon

At about age 11, Avis left her house with some books under her arm and conviction in her heart. She found herself climbing the hills of the countryside near where she lived, locating people living in poverty. Many of the people she found were totally illiterate — never having had the opportunity to go to school. For her, even at this young age, learning to read was one of the most important life skills and she was driven to teach them.

This wasn't something her mother and father instructed or expected of her; Avis was compelled, even at this early age, by an inner sense of concern for the plight of others.

"I just needed to live outside of myself to be happy," she recalls.

Avis found it difficult to imagine how people could go through life not knowing how to read and write.

"I had a strong motivation to focus on causes outside of myself," she recalls. Realizing years later that this was known as empathy, she says this is the "quintessential gift that we give to others."

"It is a matter of recognizing our common humanity — of having compassion, and being willing to commit ourselves in service to others."

Jamaica's motto is "out of many, one people." In these hills of rural Jamaica, Avis easily demonstrated this affirmation. She found many adults who hadn't had the opportunity to go to school, and so they welcomed her efforts.

To this day, Avis remembers a 65-year-old woman who could not say the word 'family' properly. "She kept saying 'fambily' no matter how hard I tried to enunciate the word for her. And I remember being so frustrated, not knowing or having the skills, to help her pronounce the word correctly."

She also recognized quite early how difficult it is to change old, entrenched habits and began to wonder if having training as a teacher would have given her the skills to address these kinds of issues.

Such vivid memories were emblematic of her wanting to make a profound difference in the lives of others at an early age. This great need to make inroads in what we now would call social justice issues utterly defined Avis from her earliest days.

As her mother offered guidance in matters of the heart and conscience, instilling high expectations on all counts, her father's role was no less important. He taught her that rewards follow honest hard work and effort, and he instructed her about the practical side of life. As a businessman, he also gave her insights into how

the world of business worked. He had a creative and entrepreneurial spirit — qualities that Avis valued tremendously and ones that
would help to define her professional life and career as a leader.

A voracious reader from her earliest years, Avis found that
her favourite books were about injustices around the globe. This
included the situation of indigenous people in North America to
apartheid in South Africa. One of the experiences she remembers
vividly is the reading of the statement attributed to the German
Lutheran Minister, Pastor Martin Niemoller, which she has
never forgotten:

> First they came for the communists, and I did not speak
> out — because I was not a communist;
>
> Then they came for the socialists, and I did not speak out
> — because I was not a socialist;
>
> Then they came for the trade unionists, and I did not
> speak out — because I was not a trade unionist;
>
> Then they came for the Jews, and I did not speak out —
> because I was not a Jew;
>
> Then they came for me — and there was no one left to
> speak out for me.

Avis recalls reflecting on this for days on end. She was haunted
by the images that this conveyed. She wondered what she could do
about this over her lifetime. Would she have behaved differently
under the circumstances? Was she courageous enough to speak
truth to power, as the saying goes? Would she have allowed fear of
reprisals to stop her from doing the right thing?

At about this time, she was reading about apartheid in South
Africa, often crying herself to sleep as she thought about the
injustice that was inherent in the system that her ancestors had

to endure. Since she grew up within a religious context, attending church, she always reflected on these teachings.

"I was a very reflective young girl," Avis recalls. "I pondered the questions of what to do, of what I wanted my life to be about. Most important to me was how would I affirm and bring out the humanity of others?"

Teacher in the Making

While Avis built a foundation in those early years as an informal teacher, her own teachers at her new school also raised the bar for her. Attending Ballard's Valley Primary School in the parish of St. Elizabeth for a short time, Avis fondly recalled the principal, Mr. Biggs, and his wife, both of whom had high expectations of their students. She had excellent teachers who prepared her well for her high school years.

Avis recalls sitting for what was then known as the "Eleven Plus Exams," which selected students for secondary school. Students who did well received "scholarships" to high school. For Avis, this meant that she would attend the picturesque, Anglican, all-girls institution known as Hampton School. It was also later known as Hampton School for Girls. Located in Malvern, Jamaica, the boarding school was ably served by Gloria Wesleygammon, who spent twenty-seven years in this role.

Avis feels she didn't do as well as she should have in high school, despite the fact that she became a recognized school leader. She did poorly in geography, for instance, and jokes that today she still gets lost wherever she goes. Although she has spent a lifetime encouraging young women to do well in math, she believes she didn't get encouragement and support herself while taking high school mathematics.

She recalls in later years the poster campaigns in Canada during the late 1970s that read "Dropping Math? Say Goodbye to 82 Occupations."

"In many countries, young women were allowed to drop math too early in their careers, and this is certainly a career-limiting move.

Avis recalls that her first career choice was to become a lawyer. "I spent so much time watching Perry Mason, trying to learn his techniques, as I wanted to be the best lawyer that one could be." As a lawyer, Avis believed she could tackle some of the social justice issues that were already resonating with her. But she would soon meet a special teacher in high school who would inspire her to change direction.

The name of the teacher was Phyllis Bogle. She taught Avis Spanish and had such an impression on her that Avis wanted to change direction from being in courtrooms to being in classrooms. What Phyllis Bogle did to impress Avis so deeply was to take a firm stand on what would now be called racism, at worst, and class bias at best.

Avis was now captivated with the idea of making a difference through teaching. She remembers thinking, "Teachers can demonstrate fairness. They can make a difference on how students think about important values — values that affect how we live our daily lives, especially in relation to others."

Unfortunately, Avis recounts one of the saddest moments of her life when it was announced that Miss Bogle was killed in a car accident very close to where Avis lived at the time in St. Elizabeth, Jamaica.

"My favourite teacher had died. The person in whom I had put my hope for a happy high school life was gone. The most fair, genuine, and values-driven teacher I had ever met — the teacher who I felt really liked me a lot and instilled in me a love of the Spanish language, was now no more."

Avis later decided to pursue studies at the university level in Spanish, this being one way that she could honour Miss Bogle's memory and the positive impact the teacher had on her life. In an amazing case of serendipity, Avis was recently in Scotland for a speaking engagement to a group of principals. As she passed by

St. Andrew's University, she remembered that Miss Bogle may have done her undergraduate degree at that institution. During the workshop with the principals, she told them about this very special teacher, Miss Phyllis Bogle, who had made such an impact on her life. She couldn't believe it when a principal came up to her after the workshop and told her that he knew her family. He later put Avis in touch with Miss Bogle's brother, a popular singer.

In responding to Avis — some 40 years later — the brother commented that his sister's life had not been in vain. He couldn't believe that after all these years, he was hearing about the incredible impact that his sister had on a young Jamaican girl.

CHAPTER TWO
EARLY LEADERSHIP LESSONS

In Jamaica at that time, "Teachers' College" was a path one could choose directly from high school. Students were groomed for the teaching profession early, and it was the path that Avis now had no doubt she would walk. What she didn't yet realize was that in 1965, Avis was one of five girls chosen from Hampton School to be the first batch of students who would start up Mandeville Teachers' College (now renamed Church Teachers' College). The college was one parish east, so Avis moved from St. Elizabeth to the town of Mandeville in Manchester. Avis soon settled in to live in Manchester for two years of studies and to hone her leadership skills. She didn't wait long to do so, rising to prominence when she was elected by her peers as its first female college president.

According to Church Teachers' College website, "other members of the academic staff at the beginning were Deaconess Winnie Hoilett, (who later became the Rev. Winnie Bolle), Mrs. Joan Swaby who taught Spanish and English, Mrs. Phyllis Bachelor, who taught Home Economics, and Mr. Kenneth Thaxter, then a Lay Reader in the Anglican Church, who taught English, Social Studies, History and Physical Education."

Aside from her family upbringing, this experience at Church Teachers' College would stay with her in important ways, with lessons about leadership foremost among them. The first acting principal of the school was Geralt Jones, a Welshman who came to Jamaica to establish this new school entity and to train some of the first groups of students who would teach in secondary schools.

Avis remembers him with great fondness and admiration for a host of reasons. He had a strong sense of fairness and believed in the ability of the students to shape the reputation and destiny of the college.

Geralt Jones would eventually write a novel (now out of print) called *The First Two Years*, which featured Avis and some of the young women from the first wave of teacher-leaders. Jones' wife, Sue Jones, taught music at the college. They also had a young daughter who was "like a little doll" and all the students wanted to play with her. Avis often wonders where she is now and if she followed in her parents' footsteps by becoming a teacher. She hopes to one day find her and her brother on one of her trips to Wales.

Recently, when she was speaking at a conference in Wales, Avis contacted Susan Jones and spoke with her on the telephone. Unfortunately, Geralt Jones, her early model of leadership excellence, had died.

During those days at teachers' college, Avis also recalls that Geralt Jones had offered to meet with her on one of her trips to New York. Indeed, he accompanied her on a tour of Columbia University when Avis mentioned to him that she was planning to include this university in her investigation of where she should continue her studies.

The Reverend Bolle was one of the first female leaders who Avis remembers with great admiration. "Deaconess," as they all called her, was a disciplinarian.

"She had high standards which we all tried to emulate," Avis recalls.

In fact, Avis believes she owes her future to the bold actions Deaconess took to make sure she had the signatures and recommendations required for someone who wanted to study administration at the Ontario Institute for Studies in Education. Were it not for Deaconess, Avis would never have received the signature which was required.

At the time, the feeling was that Avis should wait until a male lecturer pursued his master's degree.

"The sad thing is that the individual they wanted to push forward had not even applied to do post-graduate work," Avis remembers, wondering how much she would have to fortify herself against sexism and ageism in the future.

But Deaconess, against the will and wishes of a senior player, signed the forms that would make it possible for her to come to Canada to do her post-graduate studies.

Avis still has great regrets that she was not able to thank Deaconess as profusely as she wanted, for facilitating her progress on her career path. Were it not for her support, Avis would not have had the opportunity to leave Jamaica to one day study in Toronto.

As Church Teachers' College grew, it increased the number of secondary teachers and eventually became the only institution on the island that concentrated on teacher training for ages 12 through 17-plus. This demonstrates how early the Jamaican system placed a value on innovations in teacher education.

Being a Leader

As Avis reflects on the leadership lessons she learned during her two-year term as college president, having been re-elected for the second year, she recalls approaching Principal Geralt Jones with a problem that arose at the College. His response was, "Avis, how are you planning to solve this?"

"I realized then that he wanted us to take responsibility for the direction of the college, including the discipline of our colleagues. That was my first understanding of what it meant to be empowered to act. Geralt Jones emphasized to us that we must be leaders who are excellent problem solvers. We should not be dependent on the people above us to solve the problems that we can, indeed, solve, at our level." That lesson stayed with her throughout her years in educational leadership.

After trying a few things to solve the dilemma, Avis felt that it was her responsibility to report back to him to let him know what they had accomplished with their approach. "Those of us who were elected had to assume this responsibility. So I learned about collaborative leadership — or distributed leadership — at a young age. The College was very significant in shaping the views that I still hold today."

Church Teachers' College recently honoured Avis at their 50th-anniversary celebrations in early 2015 for her accomplishments. She noted during her recent visit there that the College helped her hone some of the leadership skills which had assisted her throughout her career.

"I am grateful to Church Teachers' College for its role in setting me on a path of career success. I remember with pride the love of learning, the values of hard work, determination, and concern for others that were nurtured. We pushed the boundaries of knowledge acquisition and mobilization and learned to be confident and action-oriented."

Avis said she also learned how to work effectively with others and how to get things done "for the benefit of those we serve."

"The College taught me to be both people and action-oriented. I have constantly reflected on my early experience of what leadership was all about at Church Teachers' College. Since then, I have always embraced opportunities to lead with courage and confidence."

Phyll Williams, a fellow student, teacher, and friend in high school, calls Avis "a humble giant of a woman."

"She is large not only in academia...her generosity of spirit has touched many hearts. So many of us have been the recipients of her kindness and graciousness, which continues even today."

At the 50th anniversary celebrations, says Williams, a number of past students from the so-called "first batch" met together at their alma mater. "We shared hilarious recollections and anecdotes from those early years of our college life. Avis, of course, featured in most of them."

Ruby Anderson was another colleague of Avis' from teachers' college days. She recalls Avis as "a role model who led by example."

"She was principled and fair in judgement, even with friends. I found her to be soft-spoken but resolute and she was very approachable," Anderson recalls.

In the Jamaican school system of the time, Avis spent two years at teachers' college, from 1965-67, then one year of teaching internship at Westwood High School, an all-girls' school, in 1968. When it was time for her to leave these formative years behind to pursue her Bachelor of Arts at the University of the West Indies in Mona, Jamaica, she couldn't have known at the time that she had not seen the last of Church Teachers' College.

The University of the West Indies

It was 1969 when Avis completed her internship year at Church Teachers' College in Mandeville. In the same year, the island nation had just changed from the pounds, shillings, and pence currency to its own Jamaican dollar. National Heroes' Day was also established in 1969, on the third Monday in October, to honour seven outstanding Jamaicans. These champions within their respective fields all emerged while Jamaica was under the colonial control of Britain. In their own way, they helped alter the trajectory of the island's history by challenging colonialism. The six heroes and one heroine are Marcus Garvey, Sir Alexander Bustamante, Norman Washington Manley, Samuel Sharpe, Paul Bogle, George William Gordon, and Nanny of the Maroons.

Jamaica had gained its independence in 1962, part of the sweeping decolonization in the world after the Second World War. In this context of a changed — and still changing — society, a young Avis Glaze was doing much the same thing. Emboldened by her successful years at teachers' college and her time spent honing her craft at the teacher internships, she settled down for a different kind of challenge — achieving her Bachelor of Arts (Honours) at the University of West Indies, about 25 minutes northeast of Kingston. She specialized in Spanish, with courses in French and Sociology.

While often these are the years when many students take the time to unwind and explore more social avenues of expression, Avis was cut from a different cloth. Shaped by her early home life of high expectations and encouraged along the way by formative school experiences, she was a self-described "serious student." In fact, she was described as one of the only students on campus who did not go to the "fetes," or parties. Nothing was going to get in the way of her being successful in her studies.

"I enjoyed my university years very much," she reflects. "But I didn't go to any parties. I just wasn't interested in the social aspects of life when I was there to learn. And I thought some of the young men on campus were immature back then. The young women were much more confident," she says with a laugh. "And those of us who had started on our teaching profession were quite serious. We had a strong achievement motivation."

Avis lived at an all-female residence in Mary Seacole Hall. She had a few close girlfriends, and her favourite indulgence was to offer her room as a gathering place for them to listen to music on the weekends. Remembering some of these singers still brings a smile to her face.

"I loved music and had so many LPs," she recalls. "My room was a gathering place for listening to music on a Saturday."   .

Tom Jones, Engelbert Humperdinck, Otis Redding, Roberta Flack, Nina Simone, Percy Sledge, Elvis Presley, Simon and Garfunkel, and the Everly Brothers, among others, provided the backdrop for her only escape from studies.

After achieving her three-year program at the University of the West Indies in Mona, Jamaica, Avis quickly found a job opportunity in a familiar place in 1972 – back at Church Teachers' College where she had been a student herself just five years earlier. She taught at the college for two years, remembering well her lessons in leadership from Principal Geralt Jones.

CHAPTER THREE
CANADA CALLING

After two years of teaching teachers, Avis felt it was time to pursue her Master of Education. She had her sights set on either the U.S., Canada, or England and made up her mind to decide among these three choices. In Canada's favour, the nation had always enjoyed a strong reputation in Jamaica as a caring society, with less prejudice than in other places. It is a reputation that hasn't changed. In the 1970s, although the U.S. had the highest number of Jamaicans in real terms, Canada received more than four times as many Jamaican immigrants in this decade than did England.

"I've never regretted my decision to choose Canada," reflected Avis. "One of the great strengths of this country is that, overall, immigrants feel valued. They feel that this country is open to them — that they can achieve their dreams if they are prepared to work hard."

It was the summer of 1972 when she arrived in Toronto and the weather, while not tropical, was nonetheless reassuring. She had wanted to come even earlier, but an emergency appendectomy slowed her arrival to Canada. To this day, she recalls taking her taxi from Toronto Pearson International Airport to her graduate residence at Ontario Institute for Studies in Education (OISE, which everyone pronounced oy-see), a part of the University of Toronto.

Although she had chosen Canada in large measure for its openness to immigrants, one of her first experiences suggested it was otherwise. At the airport, the border guard looked suspiciously at her student visa and her Christmas cake that she had brought to

Canada — a gift from her family. In a blatant case of stereotyping, he wanted to know if there was marijuana inside the cake and suggested that he might cut it open to find out.

"I was so angry to be subjected to that type of stereotyping," she said, "especially since I wasn't even a cigarette smoker." Wagging her finger at the customs officer, she said emphatically, "Sir, if you cut that cake then you can go ahead and eat it."

The guard let her pass, cake still intact.

In another example of 1970s' stereotyping that Avis endured was when she walked into a dress shop in downtown Toronto, only to be confronted immediately by a saleswoman who declared forcefully that "there are no dresses on sale here!"

"That was upsetting, too, and I certainly let her have it," Avis recalls.

As summer moved to fall, then winter, Avis was shocked at what was happening to the weather. The skies grew darker more often. The temperature dropped...and then snow fell. Avis had never seen snow before and remembers feeling like a little girl, marvelling at the white particles and flakes falling from the sky. Once the beauty and wonder had passed, though, reality set in.

"Winter was just awful. I didn't want to stay," she admits. "Then one day early in the winter there occurred such a clear, sunny day. I felt such joy at seeing the bright sun, and I raced outside to experience it." However, she hurried outside dressed for summer and quickly realized the Canadian winter sun was a sham. It promised much, but under delivered. She learned not to necessarily associate the sun with summer-like temperatures in her new country.

In the meantime, Avis had met many fellow students and teachers who welcomed her with open arms. There was far more to balance in Canada's favour through the majority of the people she met and the quality of the experiences that she had.

In her first winter in Canada, she remembered walking home to her residence with two full, brown paper grocery bags in her hand, the standard kind of bags that were used at the time. With her fingers so cold, as yet unaccustomed to winter, and trying to balance the bags in her arms, many of her groceries slipped from her hands. As food spilled onto the frozen sidewalk, a man who had been driving by noticed and stopped to help her gather her groceries back into her bags. Gestures like this reinforced for Avis her belief that there was a common humanity to be found in Canada, which would only grow stronger in the country with time.

Remembering early days at OISE

OISE was centrally situated at Bloor and St. George Streets in Toronto. Avis felt fortunate, given that her residence was obliquely opposite OISE. "This was a blessing because I could be there early in the morning, and stay until just before the library closed. It was an old building, but we did not mind at all. It was the perfect place if one wanted to be in the city," she said.

Avis said she loved OISE because "it was the place that turned me on to learning for the sake of learning."

"I was able to pursue my areas of deepest interest in education, conducting research papers on the topics that I wanted to investigate further."

She found the flexibility of her professors refreshing. Students could select areas to pursue in further depth and could always find a professor who would discuss possibilities to enhance their learning.

Her first master's program was in educational administration. She later did a second master's program in guidance and counselling, and further courses in special education, among others. In total, she estimates that she completed about thirty graduate courses across departments. Learning administrative theory and studying about interpersonal dynamics in leadership were themes that were of great interest to someone who wanted to be a school administrator.

"We did in-basket exercises and critiqued the behaviour of leaders. We learned what effectiveness in leadership looked like and were able to reflect on the leaders we have known in our careers, some of whom were by no means effective according to those standards. But, for the most part, we saw congruence between theory and practice and learned how to evaluate leadership effectiveness."

One of the most compelling figures for Avis during these early years at OISE was the dean of women at Victoria College, Aida Graff. For Avis, Graff demonstrated strength, courage and a keen sense of fairness in her leadership role. Graff made Avis a don — essentially a fellow or a tutor of a university, especially traditional collegiate universities like OISE. She then promoted Avis to senior don in residence at Margaret Addison Hall, giving her added responsibilities. This role complemented her doctoral studies in counselling psychology, providing opportunities for counselling experience as she worked with young women in residence with all the issues they had to confront.

"Many were from rural Ontario," Avis remembers. "Others were leaving home for the first time."

She knows that some of these young women had difficulty dealing with the new freedom they suddenly had. "It was daunting for many. But they were very bright, aware and conscientious young women with strong career orientations."

Avis often wonders where many of them are today. She imagines most of them assumed some leadership role in their organizations and communities.

As senior don in residence, the position required a "live-in" role that obliges dons to play a key role in the lives of the students, to be an active part of the community, and to be available to respond to issues as they arise. The position also provides ongoing support to students in all aspects of their university lives. The experience of working with young undergraduate women, offering counselling and support as they got used to university life, complemented Avis' own studies when she did her second master's program and doctoral studies in guidance and counselling.

Being a don made a helpful financial contribution to Avis' finances, given that she was a visa student during a time when the value of the Jamaican dollar was seriously diminished against the Canadian and U.S. dollars. The government had also hiked the fees for non-Canadian students to three times what Canadian students paid at the time.

Avis believes that when developed countries help to educate students from developing countries, they are making a significant contribution to international economic development. "It would not be farfetched to think that they may also be contributing to world peace, ultimately," she says. Avis is convinced that when individuals return to their countries, they will be positive about their experiences and will make decisions that will benefit Canada. This is one way that Canada and other wealthy nations can contribute to international development.

What Avis liked most about her days at OISE was the kindness and generosity of her professors. She recalls people like Dormer Ellis, Jack Quarter, Mary Alice Guttman, and Gerry Wine who formed her thesis committee at the doctoral level.

"John Weiser was a sage," says Avis. "He was the epitome of Rogerian philosophy in action. He modelled what it meant to be an effective listener. Dormer Ellis, who taught me the statistics that I needed to complete empirical research at the doctoral level, invited me to her home and served milk and cookies while she helped to proofread my thesis. Other professors, like Don Brundage, invited us to his home for Christmas dinner. He, and others like Ken Preuter, cared deeply about the 'visa students' who would not be able to return to their home countries at Christmas. For Avis, OISE will always be a very special institution. She loved every moment she spent there. It opened her mind to learning. She was treated very well, and she found her professors to be outstanding.

Avis felt OISE offered the flexibility that an adult model of education should offer. "At the same time, it had very high standards, and we rose above them. The bar was constantly being raised, and we soared to new heights of attainment. But what was most important is that it solidified a love of learning and a strong research orientation."

One of the highlights of Avis' career was when she was recently granted a Distinguished Educator Award by OISE, her alma mater.

"It was particularly energizing to share the stage with Don Brundage," she says, the professor who was especially kind to her, when he, too, received the same award.

Recently, Avis met with Dormer Ellis, who was visiting Vancouver. Avis picked her up at the hotel and brought her and her husband home for dinner. This allowed her to express her gratitude to Dr. Ellis in person for being such a supportive professor during her post-graduate days at OISE.

CHAPTER FOUR
DOCTORAL PROGRAM

After pursuing her masters' programs, Avis continued with her doctoral program. It was equally "enjoyable" for her — not always the choice of adjectives for many young people reaching for this milestone.

One of her many interests was in the career development of young women. The women's movement had created a profound impact. After spending an inordinate amount of time trying to think of an esoteric thesis topic, a professor gave Avis advice that she would never forget. The advice was to simply select a topic that she could relate to personally and that would hold her interest over time. In this post-women's liberation era, her many interests converged on one topic: *Factors Which Influence Career Decision Making of Young Women: Implications for Career Development.* This theme certainly held her interest from beginning to end, enabling her to finish in record time.

"This was in the wake of the women's movement, which served as a catalyst in generating interest and stimulating discussion on the status of women in general, but regarding women in the work-force in particular," Avis would later write.

"Despite the discernible increase of women in the job market at that time, occupations continued to be gender-segregated, and women were still clustered in certain careers. High-status occupations continued to be dominated by men and the salary differentials between males and females were still widening at that time."

Her literature review highlighted that there were consistent findings on the factors that influenced career choice of females. These were:

- Sex-role ideology

- Role models

- Socio-economic status

- Knowledge of the status of women in the workforce

- Family characteristics such as the education of parents, occupation of mother, the mother's employment history, and parental expectations

- Personal characteristics such as ethnicity, place of birth and number of years in Canada, position in the family, religion, self-knowledge, and exposure to a women's studies course.

Some of the findings included:

- Parents had higher expectations for their daughters than daughters had for themselves.

- The majority of girls identified with their mothers. The girls who identified with their fathers had higher career expectations.

- Both parents wanted their daughters to combine marriage and a career.

- Many girls *aspired to* non-traditional occupations but *expected* to end up in more traditional occupations.

- Those who had role models in non-traditional occupations were more likely to aspire to these occupations.

- Only 16 percent of the girls had taken a course in which they discussed women's issues.

- On the sex-role ideology scale, about a third of the girls could be described as "liberated," a third as "moderates," and the other third as "traditional." Suffice it to say that these designations had a strong relationship with career decision-making.

- The type of school that the girls attended had a strong relationship with their career aspirations and expectations.

- The variables that contributed to career commitment were: ethnicity, position in the family, the mother's feelings about employment, the parent the student most wished to emulate, and how much they knew about women in the workforce.

As she worked toward her doctorate, Avis benefited from the generosity of John and Wilma Gummow. Wilma was a member of a philanthropic educational organization (PEO), which gave Avis a small scholarship toward her tuition fees in her first year. John was director of education in Middlesex County. John made it possible for her to conduct her research on almost 1,200 girls in Grades 11, 12, and 13 for her thesis. The findings were discussed at a conference, recommended by Dormer Ellis. The newspapers picked up on the findings, and they were reported across North America.

This marked the beginning of Avis' lifelong and highly successful speaking career.

Guidance and Counselling

After serving as a special education teacher at an elementary school in the Catholic system for one year in Toronto, Avis worked as a guidance counsellor for two years in 1980 at D'Arcy McGee Middle School in the city. She did this while she was earning her doctorate, with her thesis topic foremost in her mind.

"Ever since I was a young guidance counsellor," she recalls, "I remember thinking that all the experience, knowledge, and information we provide to students in an age-related way is so important. When students see the relationship between learning and earning, it can be very motivating."

While Avis earned her doctorate in dissecting the factors that led to career aspirations of Ontario high school girls, she didn't ignore the special concerns of boys, either, when it came to career development.

"When I was a guidance counsellor, and subsequently head of a guidance department, I was equally concerned about boys' career decision-making. Boys, too, need information and experiences to ensure that they do not give in to sex-role stereotyping and that they develop self-awareness — of their interests, aptitudes, values, and dispositions — to ensure that they select occupations consistent with their interests, needs, abilities, and aspirations."

An Equity Imperative

For Avis, career development is an equity imperative. As an aspect of general education, it has the potential to enhance the roles and the life chances of students. As an instructional strategy, she believes career education has the potential to improve educational outcomes, particularly for those students at risk of dropping out of school.

"The delivery of the guidance program is the responsibility of all teachers. Teachers at all levels of the system have a tremendous impact on the career decisions that students make. They know their students well. They can visualize what they can become. They know their background, constraints, and possibilities. Because teachers spend so much time with their students, they know them from more than an academic stance. And students depend on their teachers for guidance and support in all areas, including the selection of an occupation that matches their interests, aptitudes, and values," she notes.

Teachers are also in a strategic position to assist students when they develop their Annual Education Plans. A student's choice of subjects greatly influences career decisions later on. For Avis, when teachers relate the subjects they teach to the occupations in the world of work, they open up a world of possibilities. Students who do not have regular exposure to people in a variety of occupations benefit tremendously from the insights they gain from their teachers.

"Students depend on their teachers not only for their academic preparation but also for preparation for life. Since career development refers to the development of beliefs and values, skills and aptitudes, interests, decision-making ability, and all other life-span choices and activities, all aspects of an individual's life experiences influence and become an integral part of career decision-making and planning."

Career development activities are gradual and cumulative, Avis notes, beginning in early childhood, when students learn about the many work roles in communities and the interconnectedness of workers in society. It is then they begin to explore career alternatives and ultimately to make career choices. Career education extends to the academic world into the reality of the world of work.

"Throughout our lives, we play many roles. We are students, employees, consumers, citizens and parents, to name but a few. The fulfilment of these life roles, and life chances, is dependent on education generally and career education specifically. Career education can help shape our prospects of leading productive, self-sustaining, and satisfying lives. It can rekindle our spirit and a sense of hope in the future. It has motivated some students to dream and visualize their role and a place in society. Ultimately, everyone benefits — the individuals and society as a whole. That is one of the reasons I believe so strongly that career education is not only an educational imperative, but an equity imperative. And if one believes that schools should provide equitable outcomes for students, then there must be a deliberate and intentional focus on career development. It cannot be left to chance. The future life chances of students depend on it."

CHAPTER FIVE

INNOVATIONS AND THE ROYAL COMMISSION ON LEARNING

After completing her doctorate at OISE, Avis seized every opportunity to speak at conferences. She considers it quite fortuitous that she soon met Rolland Fobert of the Ontario Ministry of Education. Rolly, as he was affectionately called, was a kind, considerate, man who was very supportive of women and minorities — something that stood out at that time. He facilitated her secondment to the Ministry as an education officer and Avis found him to be one of the most helpful individuals that she had ever met to help her along in her education journey. She has the greatest admiration for the leadership skills Rolly provided to educators in general and school counsellors in particular. It is a certainty, according to Avis, that Rolly advanced the cause of guidance and counselling in Ontario schools. Avis remembers Rolly with great admiration for giving her the opportunity of a lifetime.

"I've always considered myself fortunate to have been invited to the Ministry at that time. My experiences there were truly life changing," she said.

"I remember well his strong people-orientation and generosity. He stands out as one of the best examples of what being humane and caring looks like in the workplace. He reinforced for me the importance of these characteristics as they represent the ultimate in what a strong leader does and represents."

For Rolly, he remembers first meeting Avis while she was a student at OISE. "She struck me as a bright and articulate woman who would be a significant asset to any educational enterprise," he says. At the time, Rolly was an education officer with the Ministry of Education.

"It was my good fortune to work with Avis. It was no surprise to me to observe the many important contributions she has made to education in Ontario and the country," he says.

In 1984, Avis became vice principal of Senator O'Connor College School, a year she considers a great experience. She attributes this positive time to the "caring and competent staff" and the positive atmosphere that they created for their students. Avis also feels that the leadership qualities of the principal, Pat Gravelle, with whom she worked, played a significant role. Later on, as Avis read more about leadership, she became very interested in the topic. She pursued research about the characteristics of effective leaders and how leaders can create a legacy in terms of making a difference in the lives of the people they serve. To this day, the study of any aspect of leadership remains her favourite topic for speeches and presentations.

In reflecting on her work as a vice principal, Avis remembers a few experiences that will remain with her for the rest of her life. She remembers having a conversation with a teacher who was near retirement.

"Throughout his years in education, every night he took home the phone numbers of three students and called their parents to give them a progress report. Parents appreciated this gesture, and often it was good news that he was sharing," says Avis. This might include how one student might be improving in math or how another might be adding insights to class discussions.

"This teacher was a consummate communicator who became legendary in his ability to keep parents informed about their children's progress."

Avis points out that the importance of precise and timely feedback is an essential component of the work of New Zealand's

John Hattie, in his findings of what works in improving student achievement. Hattie wrote *Visible Learning*, a synthesis of 800 meta-analyses, covering more than 80 million students.

York Region Catholic District School Board

From 1986 to 1991, Avis served as both an assistant superintendent in the York Region Roman Catholic Separate School Board and later as a superintendent of education.

Just before those years, Ontario's deep attachment to Progressive Conservative Premier Bill Davis had ended in 1985, when he chose to retire. Davis had been highly regarded, even before he was premier. As education minister for about a decade in the 1960s, he was the founder of the entire community college system in Ontario. He oversaw the creation of five universities, the public television station TVO, and Avis' alma mater, OISE. When Davis retired, the caretaker premier, Frank Miller, took the party further to the ideological right and the electorate instead decided to award the premiership to his Liberal opponent, David Peterson. The new Liberal premier led a largely progressive government during its five years in power, aided by an agreement with the NDP under its leader, Bob Rae, for its first two years. As the national economy weakened, though, the voters grew restless. As well, the Liberal premier championed the federal government's Meech Lake Accord, which was popular with the vast majority of Canada's leadership, to accommodate Quebec's aspirations within Canada's constitution. However, it was not popular with a broad swath of so-called "ordinary" Canadians. Those politicians who supported it often paid the price. Peterson's star began to fade.

During this time of political transition, Avis moved into the senior ranks of education hierarchies in Canada's largest province. Avis well remembers Susan LaRosa, a fellow superintendent there, when they served at the same time.

"She was a very hard worker who believed strongly in implementing initiatives that would influence the culture of the system positively."

As two women in a male-dominated world at the time, Avis believes they were able to support each other. "This contributed significantly to our job satisfaction."

Susan went on to become the director of education at the York Catholic board, and Avis notes that LaRosa took the board to greater heights in student achievement.

Avis recalls not understanding why more women didn't choose to take their rightful place at decision-making tables. She couldn't fathom why they didn't seize more leadership opportunities that came their way.

"Jamaicans have a history of strong female leadership. We grew up with notable female leaders. So in Canada, I wondered what was going on. That's why I became part of the women's movement here. In my mind, there was no reason for women to be insecure and not move up the hierarchy in higher numbers."

One of the experiences that Avis valued early in her career in Canada was her stint at the Ontario Women's Directorate. "I became steeped in research on women in the workforce and wrote career development materials for students. One of these included preparing documents with the pronoun 'she' instead of 'he' in describing occupations — especially those that were considered to be 'non-traditional' for women."

This meant that in describing the work of an engineer, for example, the description would speak about the electrical engineer in terms of the job and what "she" does on a daily basis. At the time, there was research done on the importance of language in shaping thinking and Avis was determined to change this. Avis was determined to influence the career decision making and choices that young women make. For instance, the following riddle caused quite a stir at the time:

A father and his son are in a car accident. The father dies instantly, and the son is taken to the nearest hospital. The surgeon comes in and exclaims, "I can't operate on this boy."

"Why not?" the nurse asks.

"Because he's my son," the surgeon responds.

How is this possible?

The answer, of course, is that the surgeon is a woman — and the boy's mother. When asked how to explain this, though, countless people got the wrong answer during this time, never considering that the surgeon could have been a woman.

While seizing leadership opportunities came naturally to Avis, it also had the potential to cause a stir in more traditionalist circles. As a superintendent of the Catholic board in York Region, Avis planned a Professional Activity Day for teachers and decided she would like to have renowned speaker and former Ontario NDP leader, Stephen Lewis, come to speak. Lewis would later go on to become a celebrated Canadian ambassador to the United Nations, appointed by then Prime Minister Brian Mulroney.

However, many higher-ups inferred that because of Lewis' wife's stance on abortion (Michelle Lansberg, who was a newspaper columnist), Lewis might not be welcome as a speaker for their board.

Avis didn't like the explanation and persisted. "I felt so strongly that I could not, in clear conscience, disinvite this world-renowned speaker. I knew I was on my own but I was prepared for the backlash," she reflects.

In the end, the speaking engagement went off without a hitch, and Avis arranged an alternative speaker for those who didn't want to attend the talk by Lewis.

As for Lewis himself, he got to hear Avis speak a number of times over the years, after their first encounter through the

York Region Catholic District School Board, and always came away impressed.

"What distinguished her from so many others was the focus on the child," Lewis recalls. "Her colleague educators talked incessantly about systems and methodologies. Avis talked about the kids — their reactions, emotions, instincts, interests, relationships, talents, skills, families — and above all, what the future might bring."

Lewis says she "conveyed it with anecdotes and charming intensity."

"It was a tremendously refreshing contrast," says Lewis.

Pregnant Teens

In the neighbouring school system — and facing firmly held beliefs — Avis decided to create a program for pregnant teen students, so they wouldn't slip through the cracks and end up leaving high school without a diploma. The push-back within the school board structure was extremely oppositional, and even Avis' allies urged her to reconsider, telling her such a program would never fly with conservative-minded trustees.

"We wrote a paper together, advocating for this program. We knew at the time that we would have to protect young women in the system."

As it turned out, the next board meeting was overflowing with interest. The stir caused by this issue was living up to its expected hype. Avis was told by allies to steel her resolve because one of the most powerful trustees — who was known to be a particularly conservative voice on the board of trustees — was going to have a field day rejecting such a policy.

Avis held her breath when it was this trustee's turn to speak, expecting the strongest possible backlash against the policy she fervently believed in. What she got, instead, was unexpected support.

"He said that he had a daughter, and he wanted to thank me for my courage in bringing this forward," Avis notes.

"I couldn't believe it. I was ready for a battle that never happened."

The trustee's remarks seemed to reflect the surprising sentiment of the majority of board members. Another trustee helpfully pointed out to Avis that one thing she had forgotten to put in her recommendations for the program was to relax the uniform policies for pregnant teens.

Even the Archdiocese of Toronto sent a note to all Catholic school boards recommending that they develop a similar program for their districts to support pregnant teens.

"Had I been afraid, then it might never have happened. This gave me more confidence to continue to do the right thing, to advocate for others, no matter what the political implications may be. There were so many people who warned that it would be a career-limiting move to champion such a cause. They were even worried that many would question my personal morality standards. But that did not deter me. I had to make a difference for these young women. For me, that cause was more important than career advancement."

As she closed her time at York Region Catholic school board and moved to the North York Board of Education, Avis was chosen for an International Education Award in 1991 in recognition of her outstanding contribution to education.

The Royal Commission on Learning

By 1990, Ontarians had had enough of the Peterson Liberals, but they weren't about to embrace the Progressive Conservatives again just yet. Instead, they opted to make a new choice — the New Democratic Party, or NDP, with Bob Rae serving as premier.

With her profile as high as it had ever been within education circles, bolstered by several signature programs, Avis was

approached by the Rae government to be one of five commissioners to establish The Royal Commission on Learning. The other
commissioners were co-chairs Monique Begin and Gerry Caplan,
as well as Manisha Bharti and Dennis Murphy. Established on May
5, 1993, the commission's mandate was to consult with the widest
possible cross-section of Ontarians, listen to their views, and
develop a plan of action for the future of education in Ontario.
This initiative would determine a new vision and a template for
action for the education of students in Canada's largest province.

As a commissioner, Avis spent 18 months travelling across
the province and listening to the perspectives of Ontarians who
shared their vision for the future of education in Ontario. She
remembers how passionately parents, business people, and community members spoke about their expectations of a publicly-
funded education system. They wanted improvement — and with
a sense of urgency. Parents of modest means told commissioners
that they would mortgage their homes and send their children to
private schools if the public system did not improve.

The Commissioners listened to 1,400 submissions in 27 centres
across the province and examined 3,600 additional presentations.
The Commission also conducted a special youth outreach program
and reviewed relevant research from the field. Commissioners
also met with experts and scrutinized education systems from
other jurisdictions.

After their extensive public consultation, the commissioners
released their signature report, entitled *For the Love of Learning*, in
January 1995.

"Thinking back to my experience as a commissioner, I recall the
many classrooms we visited and the hundreds of Ontarians who
came to share their vision for education with us. On a few occasions, the challenges faced by children and their teachers were so
daunting that I had to wipe away tears, hoping that no one would
notice," Avis recalls.

She vividly remembers two such classrooms. The first was
a classroom she visited in a school in northern Ontario for

indigenous children. She saw how the children lived and learned more about their experiences. She talked with younger ones who did not want to leave their homes and families in remote areas to attend schools.

"I saw their tears and felt their pain and anguish."

The other classroom experience that is seared into her memory was when a Grade One teacher made a presentation to the commissioners. The teacher related to them the frustrations, challenges, and rewards she experienced on a daily basis as she worked valiantly to cope with the diversity of the needs of the children in her classroom. She talked about children from war-torn countries, children in need of protection, children who lived in abject poverty, and children for whom English was not their first language.

"In our final report, we wrote about the professionalization of teachers as one of the most important levers of improvement in the quality of schooling," says Avis.

The Commissioners wrote:

Teachers are our heroes. We believe they should be everyone's heroes.... Anyone who has watched a teacher begin a day facing a group of kids who would rather be anywhere in the world than sitting in that classroom learning about something called geometry that they couldn't care less about understands only too well what a frustrating, thankless, enervating task these mortal women and men face so much of their working lives. In return, they feel unappreciated, disrespected, the focus of attacks, caught in an almost war-like situation not to their making...

Yet just about all of us remember with love and gratitude those special teachers we encountered along the way who influenced our lives so greatly. They're still out there, the naturals, the born teachers, accomplishing miracles. We've seen teachers whose Grade 2 kids were writing real essays and happily learning about correct spelling, grammar and syntax in the process.

*... We saw with our own eyes a group of young teenage boys
— so engrossed in a computer project they were doing together
that they ignored the lunch bell. ...We've learned of teachers
who have saved kids in trouble from doing terrible damage to
their lives, and who have spent time and energy persuading
them to stay in school. We know of teachers who have given
themselves to other troubled kids and ended up with heartache
and frustration; that, too, is part of the reality.*

Avis says that as commissioners, they were quick to admit that
it would be too good to be true to expect all teachers to be dedicated, devoted, and brilliant in their work. In fact, many students
told them in no uncertain terms that there were teachers who
were "uncommunicative, unresponsive, indifferent, mechanical,
inflexible and responsible to no one."

"Some, they explained, were 'retired on the job.'"

The commissioners felt that one such teacher was one too
many. They felt that there was no excuse for poor teachers and
that those who were not doing well should receive the support
they needed to improve. "Fortunately," she added, "we did not
come across many poor teachers."

The emphasis the commissioners placed on accountability was
strong. They went as far as to say that for every student who fell
through the cracks someone should be held responsible. Today,
she would repeat one of the comments she has been known to
make: "There should be no throw-away kids."

"We need all our students to be educated based on our moral
imperative to educate the nation's children, to enhance their life-
chances, and to make our communities safe and productive. And
if we do not subscribe to the moral imperative, let's consider the
economic imperative. As a society, we must be able to pay for the
pensions of this large cohort of baby boomers."

The Royal Commission on Learning recognized four crucial
initiatives to dramatically improve education in Ontario. They
were: early childhood education, new school-community alliances,

information technology and the professionalization of teaching. The commissioners noted these four areas could be considered "engines of change."

In total, within the four-volume, 550-page report there were 167 recommendations that were made. In fact, the NDP government under Bob Rae began to immediately implement many of the recommendations.

In a look back in *Professionally Speaking Magazine*, ten years after the report was released, Avis noted that about 40 of the recommendations were addressed, in whole or in part. These included:

- annual education plans
- the four-year secondary program and secondary school reform
- curriculum review, development, and implementation
- full disclosure on student transcripts
- mandatory community service for high school students
- expansion of apprenticeship programs
- a provincial report card
- prior learning assessment
- review of the Identification, Placement and Review Committee (IPRC) process
- secondary school literacy test
- new guidelines for guidance and counselling
- student trustees on school boards
- student codes of conduct
- mandatory school councils
- establishment of the Ontario College of Teachers

- accreditation of faculties of education by the Ontario College of Teachers

- mandatory testing

- establishment of the Education Quality and Accountability Office (EQAO)

"I don't believe we left any stone unturned in the recommendations we made. In fact, I do believe that we provided a blueprint for education reform," says Avis.

Like Peterson's Liberals before them, the NDP government under Bob Rae lasted only one term as it struggled to enact its social democratic ideals while grappling with fiscal challenges. As Avis left North York Board of Education to take up a position with York Region District School Board, a sea change was also coming for the province in its political leadership.

York Region District School Board

Avis moved to the York Region District School Board — the third largest school board in Ontario and one of the most ethnically diverse. Her tenure there was from 1995 to 2002. Six of those seven years were spent as associate director of education. These were the exact same years that Ontario's Progressive Conservative government came back to power, this time under Premier Mike Harris. Harris led an ideologically more conservative strain of the party than had ever previously existed. The last significant Progressive Conservative Party leader had been the widely admired progressive, Bill Davis, who had served 14 years as premier from 1971 to 1985.

Roger Martin, writing in *The Walrus* magazine in 2009, said there was "an unprecedented disinvestment in public education" during the Harris Progressive Conservative government's years in power. Yet curiously, these years were among the most productive and progressive for Avis in York Region, not the least of which were more pioneering, signature programs. In some ways, it was about responding through board-level innovation in response to the gaps left by a void in provincial leadership on the education front.

Pat Howell, president of the Markham African Caribbean Association, was one of many people who were excited to hear that Avis would be working for York Region District School Board.

"Prior to that, I had heard so many great things about her that her appointment to this post was like music to my ears, and for many others as well."

Howell points out that over the years, Avis had already accomplished so many "incredibly positive endeavours" that shortly after her appointment to the school board, Howell extended an invitation on behalf of the Markham African Caribbean Canadian Association. She was requested to appear at a student conference as the keynote speaker.

"Her speech was inspiring and moving. Her message captivated the audience of teachers, parents, students, dignitaries, and guests," remembers Howell.

Howell recalls that Avis spoke "about her strong belief that all children can learn with proper supports and effective teaching, regardless of their background factors or personal circumstances."

Avis would soon establish a relationship with the Markham African Caribbean Canadian Association, says Howell, and "established the very generous Dr. Avis Glaze Scholarship Fund, enabling outstanding students in York Region to attend university and college."

Howell says Avis is a firm believer in the importance of building capacity to ensure all children achieve and are educated using an equitable framework. She spearheaded numerous initiatives ensuring equity in education and equal opportunity for learners all over Ontario.

Program for Expelled Students

Under the new Harris conservatives, the Ontario Safe Schools Act was introduced in 2000. It allowed schools to set mandatory suspensions or expulsions for certain transgressions, and it shifted the onus onto school principals instead of the school boards. The climate had become a "zero tolerance" environment, and it resulted in a high number of suspensions and expulsions. During the time it was in place, the Ontario Human Rights Commission found the act had a disproportionate impact on students with disabilities and black students.

Avis chose to meet with most of the students who were designated by schools to be expelled. Elected school trustees are the ones who have the legal authority to expel students. Avis was present at the expulsion hearings. She recalls one such meeting quite vividly — the expulsion of a 14-year-old boy who was below the mandatory school leaving age, who was deemed to be too violent for school life. Avis knew that most expelled students hailed from generally disadvantaged, working-class families and they needed advocates.

Eventually, a thin, teenaged boy showed up to the proceedings. He was poorly dressed, with his mother on his arm. They were from a working-class area of the region and their dress and demeanour reflected a dire need for support in a number of ways. Avis remembered feeling that poverty, in all its dimensions, was staring all of them in the face.

When it was the mother and son's turn to speak, the mother sounded desperate. "Just help me and my boy," she kept repeating over and over, Avis recalls.

Her son said, "it's just me and my mother here...we don't know what I can do now."

As Avis watched the boy be expelled, she remembers crying at the back of the room as she thought about his circumstances and those of his mother, who both clearly needed support.

"I knew at that moment I had to do something," says Avis.

That very night she went home and had the idea of putting together an outline of a program for expelled students for York Region's public school board. It was a way to keep young people in school so they wouldn't fall between the cracks of the system. She garnered the support of a few key individuals in the school district to fine tune the idea and to develop a strategy for presentation to the board of trustees. Avis recalls vividly that not all trustees were initially in favour. A few were concerned about the fact that it was their responsibility to ensure that there were safe and positive environments created to facilitate learning for the vast majority of students. She had to work hard in the background, using her influencing skills, to get the support necessary to make this program become reality.

"During a meeting with one trustee who I had to convince, I remember using the words of Barbara Coloroso, who once said, 'If they don't go through the front doors of our schools upon graduation, they may come through the back doors of our communities.'"

So many students who do not get a good education and who are illiterate eventually may end up in the justice system, Avis points out. Another popular statement that Avis quotes often is: "We either pay now or pay more later."

Avis shared her full plan with this trustee, but he told her that he wouldn't directly support her. He was more concerned about the kids who were the victims of violence — some of whom were beaten up and were in hospital.

"However, he promised to abstain from voting against the program," remembers Avis. That night, the plan for expelled students passed. Avis found a school that was slated for closing. She found some psychologists to help out with behavioural concerns for the students who would attend. She also recruited two outstanding secondary school teachers who would be the linchpins to make the new school a success for students who needed a second chance to succeed.

Staff from the York Region District School Board held two consultation sessions to discuss the idea and to build an alliance to address the issue. Their primary intention was to establish a program to enable students to leave school with a diploma and the skills necessary for success in the workplace and in life.

"We felt strongly that the fulfilment of our mission as a school district depended on such actions," recalls Avis.

Members of the consultation group included the Children's Aid Society, Probation, Parole and Corrections Services, and the police — those who were most often involved in the lives of expelled students. That's when York Region's "Alternative Classroom and Counselling for Expelled and Suspended Students" (ACCESS) program was born.

When school districts had no choice but to expel students (given the provincial legislation), particularly those of compulsory school age because of the gravity of the infraction, Avis couldn't help but feel deeply concerned.

"The long-term implications for the individual and for society as a whole was what was at stake. In establishing the ACCESS program, therefore, we were mindful of the fact that the general well-being and the quality of life we enjoy as a society is threatened when students leave school with poor levels of education," says Avis.

The ACCESS program for expelled students was created with the following key components:

- credit accumulation

- anger management counselling

- diagnostic/academic assessment

- psychological assessment

- special education modifications, if necessary

- transition to work-related programs such as cooperative education programs, as appropriate.

The location for the program was carefully selected with criteria such as accessibility and a location not associated with the regular day school.

"We chose a location near our continuing education facilities in order to enable some of the students to have access to additional programs, if necessary," recalls Avis.

There were several indicators of success for the program. These included:

- Improved academic credit accumulation

- Re-entry into the school system with greater self-confidence, positive behaviours, and the motivation to learn

- A successful transition into the workforce.

A researcher, Scott Milne, who was external to the school board at the time was engaged to evaluate the effectiveness of the program. He collected baseline data on student demographics, expectations, academic achievement, attitudes, and behaviours.

In his final report, it was evident that students preferred the ACCESS approach to education to other forms of education they had experienced. They identified reasons such as the one-on-one teaching, smaller class size, flexible work schedules and the commitment and attention provided by the teachers. The students insisted that these factors were responsible for their improved academic performance.

The researcher concluded that the success of the program was unequivocal. The credit accumulation of students was beyond expectations, and some students applied for re-admission to school within the district. Others made a successful transition to post-secondary institutions and the workforce.

A Focus on Leadership Development

In 1995, Avis was appointed superintendent of education in the York Region District School Board by Director Bill Hogarth, Chair Bill Crothers, and an outstanding group of trustees. Her primary responsibility that year was for leadership development and the board established one of the first "leadership institutes" in a school district in Canada. Avis became an associate director of education a year later and was able to continue this work with the assistance of "staff developers."

"This was very significant period in education in Ontario. Many districts were cutting programs. But in York Region, nothing appeared to be beyond possibility. Parents and communities had high expectations for progress in student learning and school and system improvement. Resources were dwindling, and expectations were exploding," Avis reflects.

Avis says she has vivid memories during this time of cutbacks. "People were looking over their shoulders to see whose department or programs would be next. There was an atmosphere of uncertainty and insecurity."

What she remembers most is that other districts were cutting back on things like professional development and other such programs that were considered to be "frills." However, York scrambled to keep these programs intact while many others "did not readily make the connection between capacity building and organizational effectiveness," says Avis.

In these settings, staff and leadership development programs were among the first on the chopping block. The York board quickly decided to do some research on its principals concerning gender, length of time in the role, anticipated time of retirement, and other demographic issues. "We wanted to hear from them what their needs were in terms of the areas they wanted us to focus on for capacity building," she explains. The study, they thought, would round off their picture of the status of leadership, the future need for individuals to assume these positions, and what succession planning should look like.

"We discovered that we would need more than 500 principals over the next ten or so years. We were all shocked. But by having the data, we were able to convince the board of trustees to maintain and increase the budget for leadership development and succession planning."

That signified the birth of what was called the Leadership Institute in the York Region District School Board. It was one of the first of its kind established in a formal, systematic, and intentional manner in a school district in Canada. It was a leadership model that began with programs, on a continuum, for those who may be interested in leadership but were not quite sure: one for aspiring leaders, an induction program for new principals, programs for those a few years into the job, and also programs in the "renewal" phase for more experienced principals.

An important component of the renewal program was overseas travel or study tours of systems in other countries. "I personally accompanied groups of leaders to countries such as England and Germany and Finland — wherever we thought there were innovative programs. Our intent was to learn with, and from, our international colleagues and to share what we were doing in York Region," Avis says.

They wanted to see the apprenticeship programs in Germany, for example. It wasn't that these programs or systems were better than Ontario's on all counts, Avis points out. It was simply that they wanted to have a system that believed in international comparability, continuous improvement, and knowing what others systems looked like and what their areas of focus were. York wanted to be on the leading edge of educational thought and practice.

"A memory I will always cherish happened during our visit to Germany. One of our highly skilled and experienced principals, who had tendered his retirement papers, woke me up on the plane on our way back home to ask if I believed that the school board would rescind his retirement papers. He said that this visit to Germany had shown him so many new ways of doing his job. He worked for another three years before finally retiring."

This was just one example that Avis recalls of the power of visiting and learning from other systems and how this can influence education practice at home.

The current York Region District School Board website indicates that the many aspects of what was started by Avis and her colleagues at the time has been preserved and, indeed, enhanced.

Board Policy #572, Leaders Development, states:

> The York Region District School Board believes that leadership development is the foundation for achieving its strategic objectives in support of the board's mission, vision, and values. The board is committed to developing leadership capacity by providing equitable and inclusive access and supports for staff learning. These learning opportunities are designed to develop the knowledge, skills and attitudes staff requires in their roles to advance student achievement and well-being.

The policy identifies the role of trustees, the director of education, superintendents, principals, and staff regarding their own learning and succession planning for the district. One aspect of the strategy that was developed years ago was the notion of "self-directed" learning and training for all employees.

"Fortunately, this has been maintained by the board in their policy, still making it possible for a principal to have some say in the activities they engage in to promote their own learning and development," says Avis.

At the time, Avis and her colleagues also began a yearly conference, not only of York Region employees, but for educators and school board employees across the globe. They wanted York Region to be the place where capacity building is valued and staff are provided with state of the art programs. The vision was also to bring together the best speakers that existed anywhere in the world.

One of the incidences Avis well remembers was that they wanted to bring the world-renowned author, John Naisbitt, who had written such books as *Megatrends* and *Megatrends 2000*, to speak at one of the early conferences. But his fee was prohibitive.

"My fear was that if this were made public, the community would be upset that we were spending so much on one speaker. But we felt that we had to set the bar high, bringing in the best in the field," says Avis.

The board organized a "Breakfast with John Naisbitt," and invited business leaders in York Region to hear him.

"We charged them a steep amount for the meal, held a book signing for Naisbitt's new book, *High Tech High Touch,* and covered the fee that he had charged."

The bar for the Quest conferences had been set.

Another vision that York had for their innovative leadership development program was to ensure that the community had access to what school board staff were learning.

"I went to Rogers Television and asked them to partner with us to broadcast our conferences simultaneously so that community members could have access to these world-class speakers. This, too, has been continued. Throughout any given year, for the past 16 years, Rogers puts on these programs so that anyone can watch or listen to these speakers. As we had intended, broadcasting our keynote speakers was one aspect of community development at its best," says Avis.

It wasn't surprising, at the time, that principals and teachers from other districts wanted to come to York Region. At one of the orientation evenings, Avis asked a few of these principals the reason was for their interest in joining the York Region District School Board.

"Many said it was because of the focus on professional learning for all staff and leadership development for those who aspired to these positions."

York Region District School Board continues to have a reputation for being a learning organization. To this day they are still seen as one of the best school districts in Canada.

"I still accompany groups from other countries who often ask me to plan educational tours for them to visit Ontario schools. So I have had the opportunity to visit York Region schools recently. I continue to be impressed with the calibre of its leaders and the effectiveness of its schools," says Avis.

Avis says she is "extremely grateful" to individuals like Bill Hogarth, then director of education, who hired her; Bill Crothers, board chair, and the outstanding group of trustees that she worked with at the time. "Their vision and openness to innovation, and their efforts to ensure that York Region District School Board become a world class organization is responsible for the place that the district occupies in education globally," she says.

Avis considers Hogarth a very special colleague and friend. "I believe that I thrived under Bill's leadership because of the qualities that he exemplified."

From an early age, Avis was interested in studying leadership and observing leaders. She knew that leadership that motivates, inspires, and encourages people to be the best that they can be is the most desirable. On the other hand, "leadership that demoralizes people, distrusts and disrespects or stifles them, is not productive in organizations or enhancing to individuals," she says.

Avis says that Hogarth hired the best people he could find and trusted them to do the work. "He is a guide on the side when needed, but he is willing to share the stage and allow people to shine. This type of leadership requires a basic generosity of spirit, kindness, genuineness, and empathy — the character attributes that we worked so hard to implement in our schools."

She found his decision making to be magnanimous and his daily interactions with people to be pleasant. "He was respectful of everyone, regardless of where they worked in the organization. He treated women leaders well at a time when many did not. What more could one ask for in a supervisor and a leader in the 1980s and 1990s?"

Avis says that her years spent in that district were some of the most productive and enjoyable of her career. "My colleagues and I were inveterate learners. When I worked there, York Region was the place to be to learn and grow as a professional. I look back with gratitude to all those who created such an engaging learning environment for students and staff."

South Africa

There was a different kind of leadership going on halfway around the world — the kind that the world only sees once in a lifetime.

A movement had been afoot during the mid-1980s in key nations to pressure for the release of Nelson Mandela, imprisoned for well over two decades for fighting against the injustices of apartheid in his homeland of South Africa. When Prime Minister Brian Mulroney came to power in Canada in 1984, he made it a priority policy of his government to press the case for Nelson Mandela's liberation, the destruction of apartheid, and the construction of a non-racially democratic society in South Africa. Mulroney also relied on his talented foreign minister, Joe Clark — himself a former prime minister — and on the stirring and persuasive new UN ambassador that he had appointed, Stephen Lewis.

After a long and sometimes acrimonious fight with the U.S. and U.K., Mulroney pushed even harder for sanctions and found allies in Australia, Zambia, and India along the way. In the end, Canada found itself on the right side of history. On February 11, 1990, Nelson Mandela walked out of prison after 27 years of incarceration. On May 10, 1994, he was inaugurated as South Africa's first democratically elected president.

In 1997, Avis was one of a small group of Canadians sent to South Africa by the Canadian International Development Agency (CIDA) at the invitation of the Nelson Mandela government. They were asked to assist with the "National Reconstruction" of the country. She recalls, with great pride, the opportunity she had to meet Mandela — something she considers a highpoint of her career.

"Meeting Nelson Mandela was certainly the highlight of my life and career," Avis reflects. As she writes, "I felt that I was in the presence of greatness. His lessons to us about magnanimity, the ability to forgive, yet to continue to fight against racism, injustice and bigotry of the greatest magnitude; the need to focus on the development of one's community as we strive to contribute to nation-building; the need to stand against racism and prejudice and, at the same time, having the grace and elegance not to be vindictive towards one's oppressors are qualities that I admire in this great leader. For me, Nelson Mandela was the embodiment of humanity at its best. Meeting him will be indelibly etched in my mind, reminding me constantly of the person I should strive to become."

Avis was very impressed with the skill level of the South Africans with whom she worked on that mission. Many had spent time in England and the United States and during that time had done post graduate degrees.

"I was surprised to see the number of PhDs — indicating that I, too, had internalized many of the prevailing stereotypes in the media about Africa. I saw a people with an indomitable spirit, boundless energy, and an unwavering desire to improve their lives and their country."

Avis says she could easily see that Nelson Mandela certainly had taken his country to new heights. "I am confident that the next generation will work to fulfil his promise of a just and equitable society."

Back in Ontario, in his seventh year in power, Premier Mike Harris resigned. Initiatives like the ACCESS program for expelled students which Avis and her colleagues initiated in York Region would expand across the province under the new Progressive Conservative Premier Ernie Eves, when he chose to implement it during his brief sixteen months in power. Despite Eves' attempt to try to soften the Progressive Conservatives' image after two terms under Harris, voters, it seemed, were looking for more than a tweak. The Conservatives were swept out of office and the Liberal Party, under education-friendly Dalton McGuinty, took over.

CHAPTER SIX
CHARACTER EDUCATION
IN CANADA

It was in Ontario's York Region where one of Avis' signature programs was given birth, one of the first of its kind in Canada to be implemented with a process that used extensive community input and support. Character education, which is often referred to as character development, was implemented district-wide here. To get there, three education forums were convened with a wide cross-section of the community, involving some 250 parents, business, educators, and religious and community leaders, reflecting on the culture that they wished to foster in schools. The forums created a space for a conversation about the role of schools in preparing citizens for the future and enabled the board to help forge a consensus on the attributes the community wanted their students to embody as future citizens.

"We convinced our participants that by focusing on our youth during these very challenging times we were helping to create the future we all wished to have," reflects Avis. "We emphasized that this initiative would also nurture characteristics identified by the business community as integral to a work ethic and prerequisites for success in the workplace."

Indeed, the Canadian model for character education was developed during this time in York Region, creating a far-reaching example of civic engagement. Uniting both educators and community stakeholders, the vision for its 27 high schools and 150 elementary schools took hold. Soon, other school boards would reach out to emulate York.

John Havercroft, then superintendent of education for the York Region District School Board, helped to drive the vision but acknowledges it was Avis that initially led it.

"The seed was taken out of the box in the fall of 1999," Havercroft recalls, led by Avis, who was then associate director of the board. Glaze and others made a presentation to the board of trustees, looking for permission to actively pursue character education.

Four years earlier, York Region District School Board could not find Canadian examples of character education. Instead, examples from the U.S. and United Kingdom were studied. After three community forums were held, says Havercroft, well over 200 community stakeholders helped craft a list of character attributes that would help define a character-based school.

"This was an important aspect of our history," Havercroft states. "That all these community partners would help form this outside the board's walls said something important about the level of community involvement we had and continue to have."

Brenda Larson, who served as editor-in-chief of the York Region Newspaper Group at the time, remembers well the community forums that were held.

"Avis is inspiring to me," says Larson, who has since moved to the U.S. and was reached at her home in North Carolina. "She's a strong, confident woman who achieved such great success in the York Region."

The former newspaper chief says Avis "makes people around her perform at a higher level."

"She could get things done by mobilizing others — and you wanted to do it," reflects Larson.

Larson sat on the Character Council, representing York Region Newspaper Group. She remembers speaking at the first community forum, talking about why her company was involved in a character development initiative.

"At the end of the day, we trusted millions of dollars in print publications and then turned distribution over to eight to twelve year olds. We had to be able to trust the character of the kids involved," and the job itself is character forming, explains Larson.

That's why the newspaper group became a "company of character" for the workplace initiative. Larson committed to the vision, running a monthly feature on character education.

The Character Council was made up of many community partners, including mayors, the chief of police, politicians, business owners, students, and others. All schools in the region had to demonstrate that they were character schools.

"Avis' influence on us was tremendous. I consider her the number one leader in character education at York Region," says Larson. "You wanted to help her...people wanted to be like her."

Larson says that perhaps the most remarkable thing is that "nothing Avis ever did was for Avis. It was for the community and the kids. She is a true servant leader."

At the end of the three sessions, the participants decided upon ten attributes that they wanted the school board to implement. These were: *Respect, Responsibility, Honesty, Integrity, Empathy, Fairness, Initiative, Perseverance, Courage,* and *Optimism.*

It was Avis' view that elected officials, particularly at the local level, play a pivotal role in the development of a civil society. And so she often reflects on how the character development program she started at York helped steer the building communities of character initiative in the overall municipality of York Region. She asked two of her colleagues, John Havercroft and Jamie Campbell, to accompany her to the office of the Mayor of Markham, Don Cousens. She asked him, and other mayors of neighbouring municipalities, to work with the school district to engage the community in an ongoing, systematic, and focused character education effort. With this coalition of community leaders, they engaged a wide cross-section of the community, including parents, educators, students, members of the business and faith communities, government officials, the police, labour and other non-profit organizations — all individuals who were interested in making the community safe, inclusive, and inviting. Students played a major role in all character development initiatives.

"Through our collective efforts, York Region became one of the first jurisdictions in Canada to develop a character initiative based on the widest possible community consultation. This also served as an example of how community development could be led by the education sector," Avis reflects.

"Schools do not simply reflect community, they can also lead community," she adds.

All nine municipalities in the region passed resolutions to be character communities.

Pat Howell, president of the Markham African Caribbean Association, says the implementation of the Character Matters campaign in York Region "introduced the concept that teaching children to be better, more well-rounded citizens was just as important as teaching them the curriculum."

"The idea that students should be taught about vital human virtues ensures that the education system will produce young people that will essentially learn to contribute to their community," Howell says.

Howell says Avis is "a phenomenal role model and a true example of an agent of evolution and change."

Businesses of Character

Avis had always believed in the role of business in supporting education. She believes strongly that the business community has a vested interest in character development programs. They depend on the school system to help nurture the qualities in their students who will ultimately graduate and work in their companies and institutions. Business leaders often say that they can develop the technical skills, but they want educators to develop qualities such as initiative, perseverance, and honesty.

The late Sandy McDonnell, a business person who had devoted his life to character education in St. Louis schools, once said:

> We in the business world don't want young people coming into our employment and into our communities who are brilliant, but dishonest; who have great intellectual knowledge, but don't really care about others; who have highly creative minds, but are irresponsible. All of us in business and the entire adult community need to do our part in helping build young people of high character. There isn't a more critical issue in education today.

In addition to winning the Distinguished Educator Award while at York Region, in 1995, Avis also won the prestigious Outstanding Educator of the Year award from Phi Delta Kappa. This was in acknowledgement of distinguished service to education and in appreciation of leadership in relating the aims, purposes, and objectives of Phi Delta Kappa to public education. A third award during this same time was bestowed by the Character Education Partnership (CEP) in Washington, D.C., which honoured her for her leadership in character development.

Towards Freedom

During this same, active time in York Region, Avis found time to co-author (along with Ken Alexander) an important textbook for students called *Towards Freedom: The African Canadian Experience*, released in 1996. Alexander was a teacher in the Peel District School Board at the time who worked in a high school with a very diverse population. They both wanted students to have a good sense of their history, Avis recalls. She admired the teacher's commitment to these issues and what he had already achieved in his school. So when Alexander approached her with the idea of writing this book, she readily saw the benefits of the convergence of ideas and mutual interest in the education of students in general and African Canadian students in particular.

"We wanted students, through the study of history, to take pride in the accomplishments of the elders. Black history was not very popular at the time. Many students had no idea of the contributions of blacks to the development of this country. We wanted them to be proud of their rich heritage and to realize that they, too, have the ability and the skills to contribution to nation building."

Avis points out that so many of these black students are born in Canada and are, in fact, Canadians. "They have no place to go back to. This is the only home that they know. And yet, so often they are made to feel that they do not belong — mainly because they may look or speak differently from their peers."

Avis has always believed that when students study their history, they develop a sense of pride in their race, background, and culture. They also develop a greater sense of confidence in their ability to make a difference in society.

One reviewer, Scott Neigh, called the book an "all-in-one look at the history of people of African descent in Canada...meant to be useful in high school classes that are seeking to probe beyond the Eurocentrism that still dominates the teaching of Canadian history in most places..." Neigh writes that the book "begins with the arrival of the first Africans to northern North America in the early 17th century and traces the path of community history through ups and downs and the consistent struggle against racism to the promising era of the mid-'90s."

The issue of the education of black students is something that concerns Avis even today. She is not surprised that there seems to be so much "unfinished business" when this topic is mentioned. Many Ontario educators will remember how passionately the Royal Commission on Learning, on which Avis served as a commissioner, addressed this issue. Avis recounts that many of the concerns, some of which were shared by other diverse groups and organizations, were voiced with a sense of urgency. Many felt that there was a crisis in the African-Canadian community in terms of the education of their students. They talked about:

- Lack of success

- Feelings of alienation

- Differential treatment

- Unfair discipline

- Stereotyping

- Bias in testing and evaluations

- Mono-cultural curriculum

- Racism

- Self-fulfilling prophecy

- Low expectations

They wanted these issues addressed with a greater sense of urgency. More specifically, they expressed their concerns as follows:

a. A disproportionate number of students are dropping out, failing, or being streamed into low academic levels or special education classes. The system is clearly not utilizing the potential of these students.

b. The curriculum is not inclusive. Students do not see themselves reflected in the curriculum — their literature, history or the achievements of their community — and when mention is made, it is often in a negative or stereo-typic manner.

c. Some teachers have low expectations of black students and expect them to fail or do poorly.

d. Strong biases still exist in psychological tests and do not take into account differences in educational, cultural, and social backgrounds.

e. Black students have few role models in the school system, and teachers trained in other countries have little access to the teaching profession.

f. Stereotyping and racism are "rampant" in the school system.

g. Too many students of African heritage are directed towards athletics and "choice-limiting" programs as a first option.

h. Police officers are called to deal with black students for even minor incidents. Often the victim, in defending himself or herself from verbal or physical assault, becomes the offender.

In short, the briefs produced by the Royal Commission on Learning suggest that many black students feel marginalized within the education system.

The briefs made a number of suggestions and recommendations, including the following:

a. The present curriculum puts very little emphasis on minority cultures and contributions. An inclusive curriculum, including black studies, is necessary for all schools and not just for those with populations of African-Canadian and other racial and ethnocultural minorities. When international languages are offered at the elementary level, black studies should also be offered.

b. More minority teachers must be hired to reflect the racial and cultural backgrounds of Ontario schools.

c. Schools and school boards should be more accountable for performance and results, and there should be better reporting of student achievement.

d. Parents should be more actively involved in the education of their children; e.g. there should be an advisory council and liaison persons to better involve and inform communities and parents. Parents should have meaningful input into policy decisions and be made to feel welcome as part of the life and decision-making within the school.

e. There should be an ombudsperson in each community to deal with minority concerns.

f. There should be mentorship programs for students, better guidance and counselling, and all students should be advised of post-secondary options. Students should not be channelled into occupational fields based on racial or gender stereotypes.

g. Teachers should be trained to identify and eliminate stereotyping and racism, to work with students from a wide range of backgrounds and be knowledgeable about Ontario's rich, diverse multicultural heritage.

h. There should be a better balance between teacher-directed instruction and child-centred learning.

It is not surprising that the commissioners made many bold recommendations, a significant number of which served as a blueprint for discussion on future action related to the issues of race and ethnocultural equity in Ontario and Canadian schools.

Avis hastens to acknowledge that there has been progress since then. Some school districts, including the Toronto District School Board, among others, have focused on this issue and have instituted professional learning programs for teachers and principals. One of Avis' responsibilities at the Ministry of Education was to co-lead the development of its race and ethnocultural education strategy, which is still being implemented in Ontario schools, with the four-year implementation timetable, outlining the responsibilities of leaders at all levels of the system. The intent was to ensure that these actions reached the students in the classroom.

But Avis still feels that much remains to be done on this front because there are still too many black students in many jurisdictions who are not reaching their full potential.

"I will only be satisfied when students from diverse backgrounds in general, and black students in particular, are achieving to the maximum of their potential and are the leaders that they have proven themselves to be in their communities," she says.

CHAPTER SEVEN
THE PETERBOROUGH YEARS

Ever since Avis left Jamaica long ago and made Canada her permanent home, she had always lived in the Greater Toronto Area. For her, Toronto was where she received much of her post-graduate education. In fact, OISE had become a new home of sorts. The Toronto area had exceptional diversity and, as one of the largest cities in North America, there was unparalleled access to career growth.

While she was thriving at York Region District School Board, in 2002 Avis heard about an unexpected career opportunity that would be outside of the Greater Toronto Area. Kawartha Pine Ridge District School Board was looking for a new director of education. While Avis was an associate director at York and had successfully worked in this environment for years, she liked the idea of leading a board as director — a challenge she hadn't yet experienced.

Peterborough is a picturesque city of 75,000, built on the Otonabee River in the Kawartha Lakes area of Ontario. It's a region known for its great cottage life during the summer months, abundant walking trails, and attention to green space. While a dynamic small city, about 140 kilometres away from Toronto, it was as different from the Canadian metropolis as one could imagine.

"I knew it was more rural than I was used to, of course," recalls Avis, "and there were many naysayers who believed I wouldn't fit in and that I wouldn't like living in a more remote, smaller city.

Moreover, many were afraid that I would experience prejudice within a smaller community."

Despite those naysayers, Avis interviewed for the position and was successful.

"They still said 'Avis, don't go!' They were worried that a black woman would find herself uncomfortable in the city. Well, luckily I was not afraid because it was one of the best experiences of my lifetime."

In fact, Avis found great acceptance and openness all across the city and county. She did at least 250 meetings and outreach opportunities in the first year alone, introducing herself and putting her own stamp on the institution.

At her new board, Avis was warned that they were not inclined to get positive press from the local media. Once a sketch of the strategic direction was set at Kawartha Pine Ridge under Avis, one of the first things she did was to visit the downtown office of Ed Arnold, the long-time editor of the Peterborough Examiner, the city's daily newspaper.

"I took our plan to him and asked what he thought — I wanted to show him the great initiatives we had developed," recalls Avis. "And I still remember him saying, "You know, you're the first director of education who has ever come to see me.""

"After that time, there was virtually no more negative press. All it took was just reaching out and demonstrating a willingness to be open and transparent," Avis says.

It also helped that Avis felt she had excellent people working in communications — Greg Kidd and Judy Malfara, among others — who demonstrated distinction in their roles.

"They helped me keep the community informed, and they believed in two-way communication as they solicited input to influence decision making."

As she and the rest of the board worked on a strategic plan that included all the people and groups in the community who might contribute, including media, she was very aware how the entire staff at the Kawartha board demonstrated a strong service ethic.

"We had major input sessions, focus groups, then came the strategic plan. It was based on true community support. We had 'scouts' trained to go around and solicit people's views. People trusted the process. There was an authenticity to it all which was powerful," she reflects.

For his part, Ed Arnold says in his "forty years at the *Examiner* few heads of government organizations had even bothered to meet with media to discuss issues and plans."

"She not only made the effort to meet with me, but followed it up and at all times listened, cooperated," and was even willing to make suggested changes, Arnold says.

Arnold says he knew right away that Avis was "someone who wanted to improve the education system for children" and "who believed in communication as a way of educating others."

She had a sincere belief that openness would help make progress, not hinder it, says Arnold, something more people in government should aspire to do. Too often his experience was that officials in many government bodies were having mostly closed-door discussions.

"She, at least in the local education board, opened them up," which was a significant change for someone in government at the time, he notes.

Avis repeated this pattern with the weekly newspaper and the local television station. She was told that wherever she went that she "had put a face to public education" in the district.

One of the other first things Avis did when she arrived was to eliminate all the preferential parking spots that the director and superintendents had.

"I took down every name — including mine, the director's. It was a sign of what the organization was going to be. As far as I was concerned, we could scrounge around for parking like everyone else had to do."

Avis says "it was a signal of privilege and I wanted to signal equity."

She points out that often senior staff were out in the field anyway, so designated parking places often sat vacant.

Diane Lloyd served as chair of the school board of trustees when Avis was director. She says that "Avis was — and is — a champion for all that we treasure about public education."

She believes in "the concept that public education is the great equalizer for all, and that all members of our community benefit from the fruits of its provision," says Lloyd. "We were lucky to have her, and she transformed our organization in innumerable ways," as Avis provided "inspired and innovative leadership."

"Her personal passion and devotion to excellence challenged us all to greater heights of commitment," Lloyd notes. Lloyd adds that under the leadership of Avis, scores not only improved, but so did attitudes.

"Avis did not put herself on a pedestal. I remember the first time I went to an event with her. Usually, the director and chair along with other dignitaries would sit at the front, give appropriate speeches, mingle, and leave. Avis started to pick up the dishes."

Angela Lloyd served as chair when Avis was selected as director of education. She has always admired Angela's leadership and is grateful to her and the trustees at the time for having selected her as director of education.

Feeling buoyant about her new leadership position and the plans in place for Kawartha Pine Ridge Public School Board, Avis decided to settle down in Peterborough and bought a beautiful condo in the city's west end.

She continued to speak at service clubs across the district, in small places like Campbellford (population 3,600) where she drew enthusiastic crowds. She says she will never forget one older man who was probably in his 80s. He approached her at the end of her talk to declare, "I feel better about education than I did 30 minutes ago."

"I was dissuaded from going to Peterborough and even smaller communities, but I have always loved people. I really believe people respond to you based on how you treat them," says Avis.

"And the people in the Peterborough area were among the kindest I've ever encountered."

Character Education

As she had taken the lead in York Region in implementing character education, Avis knew she wanted to lead a similar process at Kawartha Pine Ridge. A series of three community forums was held on the topic and represented an opportunity for a wide cross-section of the community to hear and participate in a vision that was clearly gaining momentum at the local board. About 250 invitations went out to a wide array of people from the community, including businesses, faith communities, parents, politicians, and community agency representatives. The first forum featured guest speaker Dr. Philip Fitch Vincent, who spoke on the merits of character education.

When the forums were over, Avis was astounded. At the end of the three sessions, the participants had organically decided upon the same ten attributes that they had wanted in York Region: *Respect, Responsibility, Honesty, Integrity, Empathy, Fairness, Initiative, Perseverance, Courage,* and *Optimism.*

"I couldn't believe it. This shows we can find common ground on the values we espouse within our communities," she says.

For character education to be properly implemented, she organized in-services for teachers, held a principals' conference, got student councils involved, and just generally did the smart capacity building that was needed. To create speedier implementation, five to eight teachers were trained in each school to help facilitate the infusion of character education within the curriculum, according to Avis.

"I was very pleased how it all came about, including implementation. Something like this isn't successful if you do not involve the people and create the capacity to make it all happen," she says.

Avis says the desire on the part of the community for character education was very apparent. "The readiness was amazing."

According to the board document *Character Education and Citizenship Development in KPR Schools*, character education was "a deliberate effort to nurture the universal attributes that transcend racial, religious, socio-economic, and cultural lines. It is a whole school effort to create a community characterized by such qualities as respect, responsibility, fairness, empathy or self-discipline. It represents personal management skills that are nurtured in an explicit, intentional, focused, and systematic manner. These qualities are promoted explicitly, modelled, taught, expected, celebrated, and consciously practised in everyday actions."

Ten points were also listed on the board's website as reasons for the need to support character education. These included: the duties of a teacher under the Education Act, the seminal book by Daniel Goleman called *Emotional Intelligence*, business and employers' perspectives, and the *Peaceful Communities* report on violence prevention research in the City and County of Peterborough.

When she thinks back now to its implementation, Avis says she is glad the community took on the character initiative together.

"Kids have so many influences that can negatively affect their lives. We had to say what we stand for — that this is what good citizenship looks like."

Implementing character development "helped to create community" in Ontario schools and school districts, says Avis. The inclusive nature of the initiative brought everyone together and helped them find common ground.

One community editorial in Peterborough remarked that "Dr. Glaze has catalyzed more than just a school-based initiative — she has sparked civic engagement in no small measure."

Character in the Workplace

Civic engagement was seen in action when the Kawartha Pine Ridge Board hosted a special forum at the Peterborough Naval Association called 'Creating Communities of Character.' In the spirit of working collaboratively with community partners, the forum began the process of moving the focus of character education deeper into the community. Mayors, reeves, councillors, police chiefs, First Nations chiefs, justices, and politicians were all invited to take part in this explicit example of community outreach.

Don Cousens, then mayor of Markham, who Avis had co-opted to support and help lead the initiative in that community, successfully implemented a "character community initiative" and served as the guest speaker at the forum. He and Avis had known each other well, given her former position as the associate director of education at York.

In addition to character communities, to the best of her knowledge, the Kawartha Pine Ridge District School Board was the first school district in Canada to establish a systematic and intentional "Character in the Workplace" initiative. They brought school district employees together and asked them to consider participating in a program similar to those that were being developed in the district's schools and the wider community.

Avis asked employees of the school board to volunteer to lead this initiative under her guidance. She chose a school board secretary and a member of the business department, a former custodian. The initiative introduced staff members to the common purpose of character development and assisted them in modelling and demonstrating the highest standards of character in dealing with their colleagues and with the public. The board also began to celebrate a character attribute each month and encouraged everyone working for the board to put these tenets into daily practice and to embody them in interpersonal relationships. Employees of the board assumed leadership for this initiative. One of the interesting aspects of the program was that office staff were encouraged to volunteer in schools to assist teachers and principals. Many chose to help students with reading.

She will always remember the secretary who met her in the hallway one day and said tearfully, "I wanted so much to be a teacher. This initiative is so rewarding. It has given me a taste of the profession I wanted so much for myself."

Avis believed strongly that this initiative would make a difference in the culture of the organization and in the service quality they provided for students, parents, and the community. She feels it had a positive impact on the adult culture as well as the school culture.

Project Reach

During Avis' time at Kawartha Pine Ridge District School Board, she spearheaded the Project REACH initiative, which identified 23 schools that had not been improving over time. These schools were in dire need of increased support and intervention. The principals of these schools were asked to meet once per month with the senior administrative team to identify the supports they needed, to discuss best practices to improve student achievement and to promote collegiality and professional dialogue.

Significant improvements were made with this approach. In fact, as a group, Project REACH schools showed improvement that was statistically greater than the board as a whole. These schools had an average of 13 percent more students achieving Levels 3 and 4 in Grade 3 Reading compared to the 2002 results. In writing, the Project REACH schools had 9 percent more students achieving Levels 3 and 4 in Grade 3, and 14 percent improvement in mathematics.

Project REACH schools demonstrated a 7 percent increase in the number of students receiving Special Education support and a 2 percent decrease in the number of students who were wholly exempt from writing the test. In other words, rather than preventing the lowest performing students from writing the test, more of them were given an opportunity to participate.

Avis was delighted with the Project REACH results — and so were the participating principals.

"The project had a very significant impact on our school," writes Martin Twiss, then principal of Havelock and Belmont Public School. "It has put the spotlight on literacy improvement and has focused all energies of the school and the board towards improving our student results. Increased staffing has allowed us to provide higher accountability for our students and there is reduced frustration for both students and staff as student needs are being met more easily and quickly. The additional human resources at the school brought a wealth of professional experience to help us reach all of our students. Most significantly, however, Project REACH has created an atmosphere of success, collegiality, and well-being among all of our school partners. We can see that we are really making a difference for our kids and the kids feel successful."

Maureen Running, then principal of Queen Mary Public School, writes that Project REACH enabled the school to "put our beliefs into action."

"The resources and support provided by Project REACH allow all students to get what they need to succeed at school."

For Fred Mandryk, then principal at John M. James Public School, Project REACH provided an opportunity "to address the literacy challenge facing our school community."

"The resources enabled the staff to become more effective in what they were doing. The reaffirmation of the fact that we had several students that required a slightly different and more intensive approach to reading instruction led me to focus on improving instructional practices within the context of the entire school. Becoming involved in Project REACH focused staff and parents on the importance of developing a comprehensive school improvement plan and working as a team. All the pieces of the puzzle were now on the table..." Mandryk concludes.

Project REACH was an undeniable success for Avis in the school district. It would not be the only initiative that she championed.

Champions for Youth

During her time as director, Avis visited a courtroom in Peterborough to observe what was happening with some of the young people who had been in trouble with the law and how their lives were being affected by losing their connection to school and learning. "I saw so many young people in front of the courts. I thought the school system should be able to reach out and help."

Some kids were just 14 and their school years were being thrown away, she remembers. "Rather than lock kids up and throw away the key, I felt we had to give youth a second chance. I said let's work together to see if there's something we can do."

After meeting with a district judge about possibilities, the program Champions for Youth was created. It was — and remains — a community mentoring program for youth ages 12 to 17 who have had a run-in or two with the law. The program engages students who have had difficulties and are at risk of dropping out of school, to help them to succeed academically and socially in society. Since most youth, but especially 'at risk' youth benefit from a stable and positive relationship with an adult, the program has been a great success. Youth are connected with an adult friend and mentor, and are then in a better position to realize their full potential, set attainable goals, and be a contributing member of society.

According to the board's website, "School board counsellors, community police officers and various community partners refer students for the Champions for Youth program based on their daily interactions. The youth involved are not serious offenders, but may display anti-social behaviour as a result of poor choices.

These behaviour choices will likely improve with intervention, and the assistance of a positive mentor."

The Coming Shift

Avis had been director of education for Kawartha Pine Ridge for about two and a half years when the unexpected happened. She could not have anticipated the sequence of events that would lead to a sudden career shift for her — one that would take her away from Peterborough and to a position of responsibility that would be Ontario-wide.

CHAPTER EIGHT
TAKING ON A CRUCIAL NEW ROLE

Avis was firmly embedded in Peterborough. She enjoyed her condominium that she had chosen to purchase on Cherryhill Road. She loved the city and its people, and the trustees and staff that she worked with.

"Peterborough was where all the stereotypes were dislodged. If I had been cautious — if I had never taken this position as the naysayers were recommending — I would not have experienced the satisfaction that I had in being in this community."

In 2003, a new premier took office in Ontario and pledged to fix the education debacle left behind by his Progressive Conservative predecessors, Mike Harris and Ernie Eves. Education Minister Gerard Kennedy and Premier Dalton McGuinty decided on a plan of action that would transform education in Canada's largest province.

In April of 2004, the Province announced its ambitious intent:

- Reduce class sizes from Junior Kindergarten to Grade 3;

- Amend the curriculum to put a clear focus on reading, writing, and doing math at a high level of comprehension;

- Send "turnaround teams" of experts into struggling schools;

- Provide every elementary school, for the first time, with a lead teacher in literacy and numeracy, equipped to share best practices and techniques;

- Create a new Literacy and Numeracy Secretariat that would ensure schools, teachers and students are getting the supports they need;

- Provide parents with additional resources to encourage and support reading at home; and

- Create an atmosphere of peace and stability within public education, and safety and security within schools.

It was the fifth point — the creation of a new Literacy and Numeracy Secretariat — that would dramatically alter the career trajectory of Avis Glaze.

At the same time, the government announced it would bring Michael Fullan into the inner circle as special advisor to the premier. Fullan — an international authority on educational reform — was to advise the premier on managing large-scale change.

The creation of the Literacy and Numeracy Secretariat (LNS) gelled well with Fullan's belief in the need to create large-scale capacity building. The education minister simply needed to find someone who could serve as Ontario's first chief student achievement officer and CEO of the new body to make it happen. It would need to be someone who had a high profile in education circles and who had garnered widespread respect; this person would need to have an impressive record of achievement, and the ability to mobilize others into action.

When Kennedy, the education minister, put feelers out to see if Avis would be interested in taking on this vital role, she felt privileged to have been asked and knew it was the kind of challenge to which she couldn't say no. At the same time, she wondered what the Peterborough community would think, given that she had just arrived two and a half years ago.

"What bothered me most was that people could think that I was just passing though when I accepted this opportunity. That wasn't my intention at all, which is why I bought a condo in the city," recalls Avis.

Once again, it was *Peterborough Examiner* editor, Ed Arnold, who provided perspective to the community with a strong editorial when letters were being written to the newspaper about Avis leaving the community so soon after arriving.

"The context of his editorial, for which I was very grateful," says Avis, "was 'let her go to serve the province. We've gotten five years' work out of her in 2.5 years.'"

Ed Arnold says that after first meeting Avis he "knew right away she might not be in Peterborough long because her approach was so refreshing, progressive, and long overdue."

"Her idea about education was also a philosophy that needed to be spread throughout Ontario. Her time was brief in the community, yes, and a big loss because she had made such strong strides, but it was no surprise when she left to join the Ministry. She belonged in a bigger pool to swim with those who could make change throughout the province — and her views got heard there. You can see the results in Ontario today."

Arnold says it's not that the *Peterborough Examiner* or the community wanted her to go. "While we didn't want her to leave, how could you hold her back? She was a great addition to Peterborough — a greater addition to the province."

Diane Lloyd, then chair of the Kawartha Pine Ridge District School Board, concurs. "We were lucky to have her, even for the short time we did. It is no wonder the Ministry scooped her away and no doubt that it was the best decision for all of the students in our province. The educational landscape of our school district, and this province, has been unalterably changed for the better by Avis."

As Avis accepted the education minister's offer and said goodbye to the Peterborough area, her greatest and most challenging leadership role was now before her. She recalls crying openly at the board meeting when she said goodbye. She loved Peterborough and would always remember the community fondly.

Building the Literacy and Numeracy Secretariat

When Avis took the reins of this new government entity in 2004, she knew the Secretariat had been given sweeping responsibility in Canada's largest province. Its mandate was to improve reading, writing, math, and comprehension skills, to create a foundation for future student learning and success. It was meant to drive change, and create a new way of working with the school districts to bring about an overall improvement in student achievement. It was also the responsibility of the Secretariat to provide strategic leadership in building strong linkages and alliances with system partners to support learning.

As she got ready to take on this great challenge, an unexpected honour was bestowed when Avis received the Order of Ontario in 2004, one of the Province's highest accolades. The Order of Ontario recognizes those who have enriched the lives of others by attaining the highest standards of excellence and achievement in their respective fields.

The Best and Brightest

Turning her attention to LNS, Avis knew she would need to surround herself with the best and brightest teachers across the province to fill the key roles of "student achievement officers." They would become the backbone of LNS and would be divided into regional teams to cover the great distances needed to reach all school boards. (Ontario, the most populous province in the country, is also Canada's second-largest province in area — larger than France and Spain combined.)

Once the critical cadre of student achievement officers was in place and a core team of administrative professionals was there to support them, Avis knew she could carefully add to the LNS team in the coming months. But for now, she got to work on the second order of business — engaging the unions.

With Premier Dalton McGuinty Education and Minister Gerard Kennedy having made it a priority to reboot relations with the unions when they were first elected, it was a great time to do more relationship building.

"We had come out of a long period of labour unrest and mistrust," Avis says, referring to the years of cutbacks under the provincial Progressive Conservative government.

"For me, I have always held firmly the belief that to get things done in schools you need the support of the unions. They are tremendously good at capacity building."

Avis says she remembers driving out to meet various union leaders in an effort to build their trust again.

"If anyone thinks they can improve education without the unions and the principal organizations, they are wrong," says Avis. "I knew they had to be brought on board as full partners."

Avis worked hard at building better relations by providing financial support to the unions to assist with professional development. The Ministry of Education supported this stance. It was an unprecedented period of mutual cooperation — of combined energy and focus as unions, school boards, and government moved to support the bigger vision of teaching and learning.

"When I worked with Premier McGuinty, I must say that I admired his strong focus on student achievement. He always spoke from a sense of deeply held values. He treats people well. You sense his respect and caring when you are in his presence," recalls Avis.

Avis says she will admit he was quite a "taskmaster" when it pertained to the future of Ontario's students. In the early days of the mandate, the premier would meet with his education team personally to see how the agenda was moving forward.

"His primary focus was to motivate and inspire to get the job done — I must admit that I liked him a lot," says Avis, pointing out his respect for people, his sensitivity to women's issues and his commitment to human rights.

"He certainly moved Ontario forward, putting us on the international map in terms of student achievement."

Avis says she believes McGuinty will also be remembered for his respect for teachers and the teaching profession.

"When I invited him to meet with our principals and superintendents, he came willingly and spoke to them, letting them know how he valued them and the pivotal role they play in education reform initiatives. People to this day remember how he made them feel and how he reignited their passion for education."

As the premier set the tone for a new era in education, his education minister was charged with the key role of repairing the relationship with unions — a relationship that had completely fallen off the rails during the Progressive Conservative reign of Mike Harris.

Kennedy played a key role in addressing these issues with unions, eventually winning them over with a commitment to new funding, a new approach, and a new attitude.

"Many people described Ontario as a system in crisis before Kennedy became minister," Avis recalls. "It took a lot of political acumen to change the culture and the climate at the time."

She says Kennedy was a very tough minister. "Many people were afraid of him. He was demanding and had high expectations — of himself and of others," Avis says. "But once you got to know him, you had to admire his passion for equity, for the disadvantaged, and for working to ensure that children's life chances were enhanced."

"I grew to appreciate his commitment to these issues and his unwavering dedication to excellence."

Avis worked with top-notch thinkers and dedicated civil servants while serving as head of the LNS. One of the most impressive was Michael Fullan, the premier's special advisor. She was excited to work with Fullan, given that he had always been a major source of inspiration for her career growth and development. She remembers as a young teacher, almost 40 years ago, eagerly anticipating Fullan's latest book.

"I would spend the entire weekend reading. Nothing else got done when a book of his was released. I knew it would provide new insights and new ways of looking at the world. The research was solid and there was always a stirring call to action."

Avis says the tone of Fullan's books was "informative, insightful, and inspirational."

"You wanted to get to work on Monday morning to do things differently. 'What's Worth Fighting for in the Principalship' galvanized us to focused action and created a desire to improve our schools. We have never been the same."

Avis always looks forward to sharing a stage with Fullan when they run into each other at international education conferences. "He is the thought leader that everyone wants to hear from, there's no doubt," says Avis.

She says she "cannot imagine what the field of education would be like today" without Fullan's influence.

"He has been a primary source of inspiration when the going gets rough in education, says Avis. "One of the greatest gifts he gave us as educators is the exhortation to lead, teach, learn, and relate with moral purpose."

Avis says it was a privilege to work with him during her time at the Ontario Ministry of Education. "Fullan pushes us to ask important questions such as 'how do you get the right people into leadership positions?'" He also says that truly sustaining leaders have deep personal humility and intensive professional will."

Avis notes that Fullan believes better results are achieved with a strong focus on capacity building and that job-embedded, professional learning in context provides opportunities for reflection. She also appreciates Fullan's stance that a relentless focus on student achievement is key to successful school systems.

"His ideas about positive pressure and support as major influences on school capacity and school student achievement will resonate with us throughout our careers."

Building the Literacy and Numeracy Secretariat

Since the LNS' inception, it was necessary to build consensus in the field and to provide high-quality professional development. The Secretariat first recognized the good work that was already being done and engaged their key partners in the process of improvement.

"We worked collaboratively with school boards to set ambitious targets, provide additional funding for proven strategies, and support over 270 successful local projects," says Avis.

Avis made a point of ensuring that all funding that she approved for school boards had a research component that had to be tied to research at the university levels. The strong research-orientation that she developed at OISE certainly contributed to this mindset and benefitted Ontario in many ways. One such approach was to provide an ongoing series of monographs that looked at the implications of current research for classroom practice. The monographs were called "What Works: Research into Practice,' and were written by university professors and researchers who had specific expertise in the area they were writing about. They continue to be popular and are frequently downloaded from around the world. Later, LNS would add an equally popular "capacity building" series that was largely written by their expert staff.

Avis also planned national and international conferences on literacy and numeracy to learn with, and from, its colleagues and "to ensure that we were mindful of international comparability," she says.

The organization continued to develop partnerships with teachers' federations, principals' councils, faculties of education, trustee organizations, and other groups to improve student learning.

The Secretariat also provided high-quality webcasts to promote instructional effectiveness that could be accessed by teachers and parents at any time from anywhere in the province, or world, so educators could have access to the latest thinking and expertise to improve their teaching, learning, and leadership. They can be accessed at www.curriculum.org.

In an effort to provide further support to schools, LNS embarked on an ambitious, signature program known as the Ontario Focussed Intervention Partnership (OFIP), which targeted about 800 schools that needed additional support. Student achievement officers worked with these schools to improve achievement.

As well, LNS identified so-called *Schools on the Move* across the province. These were schools, many of which operated in challenging circumstances, that were doing well academically. They were supported to share their successful practices and the lessons learned with others.

Directors of education were largely happy with the inception of the LNS. Board level leaders knew it offered a chance to move away from silos and into a big picture framework. Larry Hope, director of education for Trillium Lakelands District School Board, was one of those directors who saw the potential right away.

"When the Literacy and Numeracy Secretariat was established, many directors saw it as an opportunity for sharing, growth, and development of our system. Prior to the establishment of the Secretariat, boards generally operated independently, with very few formal ways of mobilizing and sharing the knowledge they were acquiring," Hope explains.

"Pedagogical and assessment strategies were shared minimally, and typically within — not outside of individual districts. Directors recognized the value of the Secretariat, as large-scale sharing and capacity building began almost immediately."

The Work of the Literacy and Numeracy Secretariat

The primary goal of the Secretariat was to work collaboratively with the school districts to:

- Create a renewed focus on literacy and numeracy

- Share successful practices among schools and districts

- Extend the knowledge base of the profession

- Increase capacity to support learning, and

- Engage parents, school councils, business, community members and trustees to further support the student achievement goals.

Led by Avis, LNS moved quickly to identify the key strategies needed to drive the improvement mandate. These strategies included:

1. Work with district school boards to set ambitious targets

2. Identify teams at all levels to drive continuous improvement in literacy and numeracy

3. Reduce class sizes in the primary grades to a maximum of 20 students per class by 2007-08

4. Build capacity to support student learning and achievement

5. Allocate resources to support target setting

6. Mobilize the system to provide equity in student outcome for all students

7. Embark on a process of community outreach and engagement to build support for the literacy and numeracy initiative

8. Demonstrate a commitment to research and evidence-based inquiry and decision making, and

9. Establish a growing presence on the national and international scene

Early on, the Secretariat recognized that a 'one size fits all approach' would not work. A range of strategies were implemented to reflect the requirements of the diverse needs of district boards and schools across the province. For change to happen and then be sustained, Avis recognized that it was critical to have ownership at all levels. "Top-down approaches have not proven to be effective in the long term," she says.

The Secretariat's approach was to work alongside districts and schools to provide a range of supports and build capacity for them to take ownership for their improvement efforts. LNS implemented a number of strategies that have had a positive influence on student achievement. The result was improved capacity for administrators, board, and school staff to effectively plan for improvement and to change practice, when necessary.

These strategies included:

- Hiring a highly skilled and dedicated team of curriculum specialists and instructional leaders who were the student achievement officers, to provide direct support to schools and district school boards

- Working with boards to set ambitious achievement targets and develop, implement, and monitor board improvement plans

- Providing a range of vehicles for capacity building (e.g. direct training, the aforementioned webcasts and monographs, and identifying high impact strategies)

- Providing targeted intervention to the lowest achieving schools and those that have been static in their improvement efforts

- Facilitating improvement efforts by providing district boards with financial support to initiate local improvement projects (local initiatives) that met their unique needs

- Creating a network of schools that had demonstrated continuous improvement in order to facilitate the sharing of successful practices

- Funding tutoring programs to ensure that struggling students received additional support

- Developing a "school effectiveness framework" that out-lined key components of effective schools and encouraged the notion of professional accountability;

- Creating a data analysis tool, known as "statistical neighbours," to remove excuses for low performance and to help boards and schools use data to improve student achievement

- Developing a network of district school boards (Leadership Alliance Network for Student Achievement — LANSA) which included some of the lowest achieving boards in the province and the highest achieving boards in order to identify challenges, share successful practices, and build capacity with senior leaders through professional learn-ing opportunities

Making its Mark

The work of the Literacy and Numeracy Secretariat made its mark and was soon being lauded across the world and by the Canadian Language and Literacy Network (CLLRNet), which was asked to evaluate its effectiveness.

Many key initiatives and research-informed strategies that were used to improve achievement are still in place. Hundreds of inno-vative projects now serve as a basis for sharing successful prac-tices. The Secretariat successfully engaged teachers, principals and supervisory officers in sharing ownership and responsibility for the achievement of the goals. They affirmed their successes, built goodwill, and consciously avoided a "one size fits all" philosophy.

The government's literacy and numeracy strategy achieved steady results. What is most significant is that it was done with the support of teachers, principals, superintendents, and all those who have an interest in the improvement of the system. A high level of enthusiasm and commitment was created within the field, and this was by no means accidental. It was the result of a carefully crafted strategy that was humane, yet demanding, and one that brought out the best in people to motivate, inspire and sustain improvement over time.

Pushing the Boundaries

A true iconoclast in government, Avis had little patience for bureaucracy of any kind. While a consensus builder and a team player, when it was time to act she was ready to make things happen. Political trepidation and second guessing were not part of her nature or design and she regularly pushed the boundaries to achieve what she thought was right for students and classrooms.

In the event where an initiative had already been given funding approval for classroom programs but Avis sensed some caution or backtracking, she always instructed her staff to be ready to "push the button" on approval going out from LNS.

"If I ever got the sense that there would be foot dragging but I was in a position to get something done, I would say quite truthfully 'it's gone — the email has already been sent to boards.'"

"I knew it was the right thing to do and I still believe that."

Avis worked under two education ministers during her time as CEO of the Secretariat — the aforementioned Gerard Kennedy — and Kathleen Wynne, now premier of Ontario. When Wynne was education minister, Avis and the new education leader got along very well.

Avis found her honest and empathetic and describes her as "truly congruent" in that her knowledge, values, and behaviours are integrated.

"Her courage and honesty are lessons for everyone in terms of what it means to be true to oneself," says Avis.

Wynne later became the first female premier of Ontario and the first openly gay head of a major government in Canada.

Avis says Wynne took the equity agenda to "new heights" in Ontario and Canada, making it possible to state the Province's equity vision with confidence and conviction:

> We envision an inclusive education system in Ontario in which:
>
> - All students, parents, and other members of the school community are welcomed and respected;
>
> - Every student is supported and inspired to succeed in a culture of high expectations for learning
>
> To achieve an equitable and inclusive school climate, school boards and schools will strive to ensure that all members of the school community feel safe, comfortable, and accepted. We want all staff and students to value diversity and to demonstrate respect for others and a commitment to establishing a just, caring society.

Avis says Wynne also enshrined some guiding principles in the province's education system, stating that equity and inclusive education:

- Is a foundation of excellence;

- Meets individual needs;

- Identifies and eliminates barriers;

- Promotes a sense of belonging;
- Involves the broad community;
- Builds on and enhances previous and existing initiatives;
- Is demonstrated throughout the system.

"Kathleen Wynne has taken us to the mountain top," when it comes to inclusive education and equitable school environments, says Avis. "She has stretched our thinking of what it means to have a fair and just society. Our minds can never again be small."

Black History and the Amethyst Award

In 2007, a few years into her work at LNS, Avis received another unexpected honour — to be chosen for representation on that year's official Black History legacy poster. Avis was one of only three women featured by artist Robert Small, including Her Excellency the Right Honourable Michaëlle Jean, Governor General of Canada, and Stephanie Payne, Toronto District School Board School Trustee and Community Activist.

Later that year, all of LNS was awarded the prestigious Amethyst Award, under the leadership of Avis. The award recognizes individuals and groups within the entire Ontario Public Service who have made outstanding contributions in client service, innovation, valuing people, and professional achievement.

Transition to Consultant's Path

Avis retired from the Literacy and Numeracy Secretariat in 2008, after four active years at the helm. She was soon appointed as Ontario's education commissioner and senior adviser to the minister of education for a short time before striking out with her own consulting business.

Calling her new consulting business "Edu-quest International Inc.," her consulting company offers a wide range of services internationally within the realm of education and people development. She continues to motivate and inspire educators through speaking engagements and consults with school districts, non-profit organizations, and businesses. For a time, she also took on an advisory role to the minister of education in New Zealand on national standards.

Focused on improving student achievement, leadership development, and school system improvement, Avis brings her inspiring approach to teachers, principals, system leaders, policy makers, politicians, parents, and business leaders to help realize their potential in improving their schools.

Avis also focused on co-authoring a number of books and articles since the establishment of her consulting company, including *Breaking Barriers: Excellence and Equity for All*, addressing high-impact strategies to improve education systems. Her most recent co-authored book, *High School Graduation: K-12 Strategies that Work*, identifies research-informed strategies to improve graduation rates for all students regardless of socio-economic or other social or demographic factors.

Filling her passport from travel to more than 40 different countries and states, Avis has taken on a huge amount of international work. One country she has visited several times to do work on a wide range of education topics is Scotland. She was honoured to receive the Robert Owen Award here, the first of its kind offered in the country.

Signs of Effectiveness

In her work as a consultant, a few years ago Avis was asked to evaluate a program at a board of education in eastern Ontario. She asked to run focus groups with educators, community groups, and students. She even had a particularly young group of seven to nine year olds at one point. As she interacted with these young students, she asked a little boy, 'What did you like most about school this year?'"

The little boy didn't hesitate. For him, it was a play called *Danny, King of the Basement*, put on by the Elementary Teachers Federation of Ontario (ETFO). It was a play that helped elementary students and teachers understand and cope with child and family poverty, along with other social issues.

Avis immediately recalled the funding that she had green-lit from the Literacy and Numeracy Secretariat years ago to ETFO for an initiative called "The ETFO Education and Poverty Project." The centrepiece was to be a play known as *Danny, King of the Basement*, which would tell the story of a young boy whose spirit helps triumph over the challenges of homelessness, not to mention life in a single-parent household.

"I felt so vindicated to have trusted the unions," says Avis. "The money we had given them had percolated down to the school level and here was wonderful proof — a young boy telling me about his favourite moment in the school year. How much more could we have wanted?"

This reinforced her belief in the role of unions to help with school improvement initiatives.

Getting Married

While growing up, Avis had no plans to get married. She was extremely focused on having a career and doing her best at it. In fact, she was afraid of marriage. She had seen so many women who had considerable conflicts as they tried to balance marriage with a career. Many had to forgo promotions because of competition or lack of support at home. But when she met Peter Bailey, an engineer who came from Exeter, England as a young man, and who had spent most of his career with IBM, she found that he was very supportive of her career and not at all insecure.

"Many of my friends were surprised at how much freedom and leeway I have to pursue my career," says Avis. "That's just the kind of person Peter is."

Avis says Peter "is the brightest person I know."

"He reads profusely and is very knowledgeable and well informed. His is on the right side of social issues. I value tremendously his support and his ability to keep me on the right track."

For Peter, there is a mutual feeling of strong partnership. "I admire her strong work ethic, and her tenacity and perseverance," says Peter, who wants her to continue to influence educators across the globe.

He once told Avis that she has "no sense of danger" and that he knows she would confront anyone based on her social conscience and strong human rights orientation — qualities he admires in her.

Peter is convinced that the places where Avis has worked are never the same when she leaves. "She enjoys working alongside people to help them reach new heights of achievement."

The Just Society

Through her many years of global advocacy for students and education, Avis continues her international outreach through speaking engagements, workshops, and as an adviser. In the summer of 2016, she was named as one of ten expert international education advisers for the government of Scotland. Avis and the rest of the panel of internationally renowned experts will advise the Scottish government on improvements to the nation's education system and on lessons that can be learned from other countries.

Avis says she feels privileged to be appointed. "I am honoured. And what I like most about Scotland is that they already have a very progressive educational system. But they do not rest on their laurels. They are not arrogant. They believe in continuous improvement."

Continuous improvement runs deeply within the life story of Avis Glaze, too. There are many ways to view such a story. There is the young girl with finely honed character, driven to teach others to read. There is the successful Canadian immigrant, determined to engage in social purpose work. There is the seasoned leader who has taken on the cause of nation building, one student, one teacher, and one system at a time. There is the mentor, who has never forgotten those men and women who were there for her as her own life path developed.

In truth, the story of Avis Glaze is all of these things and more. Perhaps it is the latter that she would identify most with now, for as global as her reach has become there is nothing as satisfying to her as offering guidance and time to a younger person. It is in this understanding of Avis that we are perhaps closest to truly knowing her best. Through this same lens, we understand that she believes in the inherent goodness of people and that her pursuit of equity for others is not borne of a misplaced idealism but rather emanates from an inner belief in what Canadian Prime Minister Pierre Trudeau called "the just society."

Trudeau explained this vision here:

> The Just Society will be one in which the rights of minorities will be safe from the whims of intolerant majorities. The Just Society will be one in which those regions and groups which have not fully shared in the country's affluence will be given a better opportunity. The Just Society will be one where such urban problems as housing and pollution will be attacked through the application of new knowledge and new techniques. The Just Society will be one in which our (indigenous) populations will be encouraged to assume the full rights of citizenship through policies which will give them both greater responsibility for their own future and more meaningful equality of

opportunity. The Just Society will be a united Canada, united because all of its citizens will be actively involved in the development of a country where equality of opportunity is ensured and individuals are permitted to fulfil themselves in the fashion they judge best.

For Avis, though, her idealism about creating the just society is always tempered with reality. That's why she speaks of equity — but only with excellence. That's why she talks of student learning — but only with high expectations. It is why she counsels patience — and yet knows that the children cannot wait.

Avis Glaze on
Educating for Success

EDUCATING AMERICA'S YOUTH FOR SUCCESS IN THE GLOBAL ARENA

The Aspen Institute Congressional Program
Banff, Alberta, Canada
August 15-20, 2011

Improving Student Achievement, K–12: Lessons from Ontario, Canada

Dr. Avis Glaze
President, Edu-quest International Inc.
August 15, 2011

PREAMBLE

In countries across the globe, from the Caribbean to Singapore, there is a cacophony of voices demanding improvement in the quality of education. Leaders from industry, business, and labour, as well as parents and policy makers, are asking their governments to ensure increasing success for all students, regardless of background or personal circumstances. Demands for greater accountability in our investment in education are reverberating as politicians make promises to constituents to bring about urgent change.

While extolling the virtues of a good education, it is also important to recognize the impact of its absence. Many years ago, Henry Levin (1972) identified in a report to Congress the cost to a nation of inadequate education:

- foregone national income

- foregone tax revenues for the support of government services

- increased demand for social services

- increased crime

- reduced political participation

- reduced intergovernmental mobility

- poorer levels of health

Numerous reports since then have shown that the investment in education improves psychological, social, and economic conditions, not just for individuals but for society as a whole (e.g., Wilkinson & Pickett, 2009). Additionally, research has shown that the challenge to improve education outcomes is achievable in a relatively short period of time. We now know that we can, through targeted efforts and innovative programs, raise the bar for all students and close achievement gaps once thought to be intractable.

THE ONTARIO EXAMPLE

In 2007, based on comparative assessments of student achievement on international tests, Ontario was ranked as one of the top ten high-performing school systems in the world (Barber & Mourshed, 2007). In 2010, the researchers conducted a follow-up study, which showed that Ontario, along with four other jurisdictions (Singapore, Hong Kong, South Korea, and Saxony, Germany), was able to sustain the gains they had made to improve student success. Ontario was identified as a "great system" (Mourshed, Chijioke & Barber, 2010). According to OECD, as well, Ontario is considered across the world as one of the fastest improving systems. What makes Ontario such an exciting international example is that not too long ago it was considered by many to be a system in crisis.

This paper provides an overview of the Ontario example as a way of illuminating what might work in other jurisdictions. Specifically, it seeks to answer three questions:

1. Are there policies and strategies that Canada is using, both in common with many other high-achieving countries and unique to Canada, that are applicable to the U.S.?

2. Are there innovations on the horizon that are especially promising?

3. What policies have been put in place to educate Ontario's immigrant populations?

BACKGROUND

Canada is one of the few countries in the industrialized world without a national department of education; there are, rather, 13 different education systems for each of our provinces and territories. Some aspects of education governance are, however, determined centrally. For example, the Indian Act gives the federal government responsibility for Aboriginal education on reserves, while the Constitution protects the rights of minorities. Catholics are considered a minority under the Constitution, with the right to operate their own publicly funded education system. The Constitution also protects minorities of the two official languages, English and French, to operate English- and French-language district school boards.

Ontario, with over 1 million square kilometres of land, is the home to 40% of Canada's 35 million people. It is certainly the most populous province in Canada and is the most diverse, home to 60 % of the 225,000 immigrants who come to Canada annually. Ontario has 2.1 million students in four provincially operated education governance systems: English public, English Catholic, French public, and French Catholic. About 4.5 % is French speaking.

From the Ministry of Education Website (www.edu.gov.on.ca)
– 2011:

- Approximately 1.4 million students attend Ontario's 4000 elementary schools

- Approximately 700,000 attend more than 850 secondary schools.

The following information is from the 2006 Statistics Canada census (http:www12.statcan.gc.ca):

- 68.4% of Ontario's population's mother tongue is English only.

- 4.1% of Ontario's population's mother tongue is French only.

- 26.1% of Ontario's population's mother tongue is a non-official language only.

- 84.9% of Ontario's population speaks English and/or French most often at home.

- 15.1% of Ontario's population speaks a non-official language most often at home.

- 28.3% of Ontario's population are immigrants.

- 4.8% of Ontario's population are recent (arrived in the last five years) immigrants.

- 22.8% of Ontario's population are visible minorities.

There are approximately 126,000 unionized teaching and support staff, in approximately 5,000 schools. There are 72 school districts, plus 30 school authorities. School boards range widely in size and geography, from a few hundred students in rural and remote areas to large urban districts such as the Toronto District

School Board with 250,000 students. As well, there are six school sites for deaf, blind, and severely learning-disabled students run directly by the provincial ministry of education.

TURNING THE SYSTEM AROUND

In 2003, when Ontario's current premier, Dalton McGuinty, came into office, he inherited a broken system. Labour unrest and tension-filled relationships between the provincial government and Ontario educators led to the erosion of confidence in the public system and low morale among teachers. The times were described as turbulent, at best. Many educators felt that there was a climate of fear and resentment, with teachers experiencing a range of emotions — from anger to despair. The teaching profession itself suffered from a damaged self-concept. Many chose to retire as soon as they possibly could. Fewer individuals wanted to enter the teaching profession or to assume leadership positions. Not surprisingly, student achievement had flat-lined, and enrolment in private schools was on the rise. From all accounts, the system was in a state of crisis.

Premier McGuinty, working closely with his then education minister Gerard Kennedy, made improvement in publicly funded education the centrepiece of the government's mandate. The first step in realizing excellence was to require that every elementary student develops effective skills in reading, writing, and mathematics by Grade 6 (about age 12). They also set a provincial standard, namely – 75 % of Ontario students should, with the right supports, be able to achieve level 3 (equivalent to a B) on provincial assessments in these areas. A provincial standard was also set for high school graduation; with adequate programming and support, 85 % of Ontario students should be able to graduate. Then with the consultation of leading researchers, policy makers, and practitioners, they evolved a strategy (see "System on the Move" for an overview). The moral imperative of the teaching profession and the fact that teachers make a difference to the life choices and chances of students was emphasized.

Key components included:

1. A small number of ambitious goals

2. A guiding coalition to drive and support change

3. High standards and expectations, with a focus on both excellence and equity

4. Investment in capacity building at all levels of the system, with an emphasis on instructional effectiveness

5. Investment in leadership development

6. Using high-impact strategies to improve achievement

7. Using data and enhanced assessment to improve practice

8. Using non-punitive interventions to improve low-performing schools

9. Paying attention to the distracters, such as collective agreements and unnecessary bureaucracy, to protect the focus on the core priorities

I had the distinct honor of being appointed the government of Ontario's first Chief Student Achievement Officer and CEO of the Literacy and Numeracy Secretariat, which I was asked to establish to drive change and achieve results with a sense of urgency.

Ontario has been able to achieve excellent results without punitive measures or the ranking of schools. We have created conditions to ensure that people develop the capacity and the motivation required to deliver on the education agenda. In Ontario, teachers and principals now feel that they have the skill, the will, and the determination to take a system to the zenith of its possibilities. And by Ontario's own standards, progress is transparent:

- The number of students meeting or exceeding the provincial standard for Grade 6 reading, writing, and mathematics has increased from 54 percent in 2003 to 68 percent in 2010.

- The number of elementary schools with large percentages of children achieving well below the provincial standard has decreased from 250 schools in 2006 to 126 in the current year.

- Secondary school graduation rates have increased from 68 % in 2004 to 79 % in 2009, representing more than 52,000 additional students graduating from high school than they would have if rates had remained the same.

- Significant learning gains have been made by English-language learners and students with special needs.

QUESTION 1

Are there policies and strategies that Ontario, Canada is using, both in common with many other high-achieving countries and unique to Canada, that are applicable to the U.S.?

COMMON BEST PRACTICES, SHARED LESSONS

Internationally, there are many educational systems that are realizing great success in improving student achievement for all students. McKinsey and Company, cited at the beginning of this paper, studied 25 of the world's school systems, including 10 of the highest performing. They examined characteristics that these top performers had in common and strategies they used to improve student achievement. Three key factors were:

- Getting the right people to become teachers

- Developing them into effective instructors

- Ensuring the system is available to deliver the best possible instruction for every child

As well, they identified the following lessons learned:

- **Lesson #1:** The quality of an educational system cannot exceed the quality of its teachers
- **Lesson #2:** The only way to improve outcomes is to improve instruction
- **Lesson #3:** High performance requires every student to succeed
- **Lesson #4:** Great leadership at school level is a key enabling factor

Ontario's demographics are also similar to many jurisdictions in the United States. We have similar concerns, including the reality of issues such as poverty and the educational achievement of students of minority backgrounds, including those of African and Spanish-speaking heritage.

The Literacy and Numeracy Secretariat

The primary goal of Ontario's Literacy and Numeracy Secretariat, established in 2003, was to work collaboratively with the school districts to:

- Focus on students, their engagement, and their achievement
- Create a renewed focus on literacy and numeracy
- Improve instructional effectiveness

- Share promising practices among schools and districts

- Extend the knowledge base of the profession

- Increase capacity to support learning

- Engage parents, school councils, business, community members, and trustees to further support our student achievement goals

Early on, the Secretariat recognized that a "one size fits all" approach would not work. A range of strategies was implemented to recognize the diverse needs of district school boards and schools across the province. The result was improved student achievement and increased capacity for administrators, boards, and school staff to effectively plan for improvement and to change practice, when necessary.

These strategies included:

- Hiring a highly skilled and dedicated team of curriculum specialists and instructional leaders as "Student Achievement Officers" to provide direct support to schools and district school boards

- Working with boards to set ambitious targets and develop, implement, and monitor board improvement plans

- Embedding a strong research orientation, conducting research, and using research-informed strategies

- Providing a range of vehicles for capacity building (e.g., direct training, webcasts, monographs outlining high-impact strategies)

- Funding "local initiatives" that resulted in hundreds of innovative projects being implemented that now serve as a basis for sharing of successful practices

- Providing targeted interventions to the lowest achieving schools and those that have been static in their improvement (OFIP)

- Facilitating improvement efforts by providing district school boards with financial support to initiative local improvement projects (local initiatives) that met their unique needs

- Creating a network of schools that had demonstrated continuous improvement in order to facilitate the sharing of successful practices (Schools on the Move)

- Implementing character education programs in school districts

- Funding tutoring programs to ensure that struggling students received additional support

- Developing a School Effectiveness Framework that outlined key components of effective schools and encouraged the notion of professional accountability

- Creating a data analysis tool, known as "Statistical Neighbours," to assist boards and schools use data to improve student achievement

- Developing a network of district school boards that included some of the lowest- and highest-achieving boards in the province to identify challenges, share successful practices, and build capacity

Ministry documents state that in order to improve outcomes at the secondary school level the government launched the "Student Success, Learning to 18" strategy and supported it with policy, legislation, and monetary and human resources. The goal was to identify innovative ways to evolve traditional high school practices in order to improve support for students while they were at school and to create the conditions for their successful graduation and transition to postsecondary destinations. Every school board received funding for a dedicated "Student Success Leader" and was provided with an annual budget. A new in-school role was also introduced, that of a "Student Success Teacher," funded above the grants that school boards normally received based on the number of students enrolled. These teachers were intended to serve as advocates for students deemed to be "at risk," to track, counsel, and work on behalf of these students to optimize their chances of success. There were further investments in leadership at the classroom and student level, provision of new and varied learning opportunities for students, including expanded co-op, Specialist High Skills Major, and dual credits.

Three themes shaped the secondary (high school) reform effort in Ontario:

1. The importance of building foundational skills in literacy and numeracy

2. The need to provide a more explicit and richer menu of programs

3. The necessity of attending to the individual well-being of students as a precursor to achievement.

The increasing capacity of Ontario students of all backgrounds to achieve the provincial standard in reading, writing, and mathematics and to graduate from high school took root in the work of the Secretariat and Student Success initiative. Both built capacity of teachers and school leaders, supported collaboration across schools and school districts, and introduced powerful instructional practices through research monographs, webcasts and web conferences, face-to-face professional learning, and a new cohort of student achievement officers and student success leaders and teachers.

Question 2

Are there innovations on the horizon that are especially promising?

In our work in Ontario, we implemented a number of innovative strategies that were key to the success achieved in the province. Each district and school had unique needs that required a range of supports for improvement to happen.

Some of the key innovations included:

- The Ontario Focused Intervention Partnership (OFIP)

- The School Effectiveness Framework

- Statistical Neighbours

- Schools on the Move

- Specialist High Skills Major

- Pathways to Education Canada

- Leading Student Achievement Project, including all principals' associations working together to improve their practice

Several of these innovations are explained in more detail below (website links are provided in the References and Resources at the end of the paper).

ONTARIO FOCUSED INTERVENTION PARTNERSHIP

In order to take part in the OFIP strategy, for example, schools were expected to put in place some "non-negotiables" to drive change. Those included:

- Developing opportunities for collaborative work at the school level and across schools

- Establishing uninterrupted blocks of time for literacy and numeracy

- Using student achievement information to determine strengths and areas for improvement

- Utilizing common assessment strategies

- Creating a school improvement team that conducted a school self-assessment in order to examine data, identify instructional interventions, and plan for next steps

- Setting ambitious achievement targets

- Acquiring resources to implement a comprehensive literacy and numeracy program

- Developing a process to regularly monitor the growth and progress of specific students to ensure equity of outcomes

- Providing interventions for struggling students

- Implementing strategies for communicating and celebrating progress

The key to success in the OFIP strategy was the consistent implementation of a few key strategies and time for staff to work together with a specific focus. In working with these schools, we learned a number of valuable lessons:

- Targeted support and focused intervention works.

- Capacity building is paramount to success.

- It was important for teachers to understand what the assessment data meant in relation to classroom practice, began to "unpack," and focussed on the big "reading for meaning" expectations to push high-level, critical thinking.

- Staff need to have time to come together regularly for job-embedded professional learning.

- Setting high expectations for all students is critical to success.

- Setting ambitious school achievement targets raises expectations and helps achieve goals.

- Consistency in the implementation of high-impact instructional strategies is a must.

- School staff should share in the responsibility of school improvement and monitoring of progress.

- Parental and community engagement are essential for success.

THE SCHOOL EFFECTIVENESS FRAMEWORK

One of the most powerful strategies and one that yielded a great deal of positive feedback from the field was the implementation of the "School Effectiveness Framework." This is a tool to assist schools and boards in identifying strengths, areas that need further attention, and next steps to be implemented. The framework helps guide discussions and move staff forward in identifying the evidence for those practices that are working well and those areas where there is a lack of evidence for specific indicators of school effectiveness. The framework is based on a philosophy of shared commitment and collegiality. It is important for schools to be able to articulate what is working well and sustain those good practices. Equally important is to identify areas in need of further attention and next steps for improvement. The process of school self-assessment provides a comprehensive look at schools, assisting in identifying current priorities, areas to target resources, determine capacity building needs, and focus improvement planning.

PATHWAYS TO EDUCATION CANADA

Pathways is an inner-city program that is achieving marked success in reducing the dropout rate for disadvantaged high school students. Its intent is to step up the fight against poverty by changing a culture of defeatism to a school-going culture among at-risk youth. Since this program began in 2001, the graduation rate for participating students has jumped to four in five from just one in five. This program revolves around four pillars of student success — tutoring, mentoring, coaching, and financial assistance. The program also meshes with the Ontario government's plan to build a knowledge-based economy.

STATISTICAL NEIGHBOURS

Ontario Statistical Neighbours (OSN) is an innovative tool that enabled us to access school performance, program, and contextual data, providing a robust picture of the confluence of factors that influence achievement. Using the OSN tool, we were able to examine school performance data and contextual data, such as the percentage of students living in low-income households, those whose first language was not the language of instruction, and those with special education needs. It was also possible to gather information about school programs and demographics. Having the data allowed us to remove the excuses for low performance in schools in challenging circumstances.

Question 3

What policies have been put in place to educate Ontario's immigrant populations?

In Canada, we have a rich tradition of commitment to justice and fairness. We were the first country in the world to embrace multiculturalism as an official policy and our human rights legislation enshrines protection for those who are most vulnerable.

LEGISLATION PERTAINING TO IMMIGRANT STUDENTS

Recognizing the importance of education, the Ontario government has established three core priorities:

- High levels of student achievement

- Reduced gaps in student achievement

- Increased public confidence in publicly funded education

An equitable, inclusive education system is fundamental to achieving these core priorities and is recognized internationally as critical to delivering a high-quality education for all learners" (Policy/Program Memorandum No. 119 "Developing and Implementing equity and inclusive education policies in Ontario Schools," June 24, 2009).

POLICIES AND PROCEDURES FOR
ENGLISH LANGUAGE LEARNERS

The Ontario policy to support English language learners provides a framework to ensure a consistent approach to the provision of supports and programs, while also affording flexibility to school boards to meet their local needs. The policy assists school boards in meeting these needs by:

- Providing a definition of English language learners

- Describing effective procedures for reception, orientation, placement and programming for English language learners, in order to accelerate their acquisition of English for academic purposes

- Describing procedures for initial and on-going assessment of English language learners and for reporting to parents

- Clarifying procedures for the identification of English language learners who are to participate in large-scale assessments

- Defining the roles and responsibilities of teachers and administrators and providing opportunities for them to develop the skills they need to support English language learners effectively

- Clarifying procedures for collecting data related to English language learners and for monitoring and tracking their progress, to support public accountability

- Describing procedures designed to support increased credit accumulation, graduation rates, and post-secondary enrolment among English language learners ("English Language Learners: ESL and ELD Programs and Services: Policies and Procedures for Ontario's Elementary and Secondary Schools")

FUNDING TO SUPPORT IMMIGRANT STUDENTS

Ontario's curriculum requires that students develop strong English- or French-language skills. The cultural and linguistic diversity of Ontario's population means that many students require extra help to develop proficiency in their language of instruction. These students include those who are recent immigrants to Canada and students who live in homes where the first language spoken is neither English nor French. Two components of the Language Grant provide school boards with the resources to meet the needs of these students. English-language school boards receive the English as a Second Language/ English Literacy Development (ESL/ELD) component. French language boards receive the Perfectionnement du français (PDF) and the Actualisation linguistique en français (ALF) components (Education Funding Technical Paper 2011-2012)

Section 49.1 was added to the Ontario Education Act in 1993 to ensure that children who are minors are not denied an education because of their immigration status or that of their parents (PPM 136 "Clarification of Section 49.1 of the Education: Education of Persons Unlawfully in Canada.")

ONTARIO'S CONTRIBUTION TO THE EQUITY DISCUSSION

The Ontario Ministry of Education released *Realizing the Promise of Diversity: Ontario's Equity and Inclusive Education Strategy* in 2009. Kathleen Wynne, then Minister of Education, asked that we draw on our experience and on research that tells us that student achievement will improve when barriers to inclusion are identified and removed and when all students are respected and see themselves reflected in their learning and their environment. She quoted equity advocate Professor George Dei by stressing the point that inclusion is not about bringing people into what already exists; it is about making a new space, a better space for everyone.

Ontario's equity strategy highlights the need for action by articulating the tasks educators at all levels of the system must undertake to make the school system a truly equitable one. The guiding principles state that an equitable and inclusive education:

- Is a foundation for excellence

- Meets individual needs

- Identifies and eliminates barriers

- Promotes a sense of belonging

- Involves the broad community

- Builds on and enhances previous and existing initiatives

- Is demonstrated throughout the system

KEY RECOMMENDATIONS BASED ON
THE ONTARIO EXAMPLE

1. Establish a mechanism to build consensus around the need for improvement in student achievement and fully engage stakeholders in sharing the mandate to improve their schools.

2. Identify one or two key areas of focus, such as literacy and numeracy, set SMART goals with ambitious and achievable targets, and stay the course until success is realized.

3. Knowing that schools will not improve without the cooperation, will, skills, and commitment of teachers and principals, devise strategies that will assure their buy-in to an improvement strategy.

4. Reduce the administrative workload of principals and teachers in a paper-driven environment to ensure that they spend more time on doing the work, namely, focusing on working students and fostering collaborative enquiry with their colleagues.

5. Develop a comprehensive, school-based program of capacity building to embed the strategies for improvement.

6. Identify and implement the research-informed, high-impact strategies that have been proven to be effective in improving schools' and student achievement.

7. Facilitate and develop a culture of sharing successful practices and the development of networks for learning across schools and districts.

8. Unpack the lessons learned and insights gained from across the globe about what effective implementation entails and utilize them to improve student achievement.

9. Collaboratively develop a process for monitoring performance and achievement at various stages of the implementation process.

10. Have mechanisms in place to monitor instructional effectiveness, with a focus on improving student achievement.

11. Provide targeted supports for low-performing schools.

12. Implement a systematic, high-quality principal development programs to ensure high-quality leadership.

13. Devise a framework to assess school effectiveness, paying particular attention to variables such as school culture, assessment strategies, student engagement, parental engagement, and equity of outcomes.

14. Strengthen opportunities for students to learn higher-order critical thinking and 21st-century skills.

15. Ensure that there are early intervention programs for students who are falling through the cracks.

16. Introduce a turnaround strategy for failing schools.

17. Allocate resources strategically to support improvement goals.

18. Utilize Critical Friends from across the globe to challenge thinking, examine practices and to provide international perspectives on the high impact, transferrable strategies that improve student achievement.

19. Identify early signs of progress, validate efforts, and celebrate success.

REFERENCES AND RESOURCES

Barber, Michael & Mourshed, Mona. (2007). *How the World's Best-Performing School Systems Come Out on Top.* McKinsey & Company. www.mckinsey.com.

Campbell, Carol; Fullan, Michael; & Glaze, Avis. (2006). *Unlocking Potential for Learning: Effective District-Wide Strategies to Raise Student Achievement*. Ontario Ministry of Education. Queen's Printer for Ontario.

Curran, Ruth; Balfanz, Robert; & Herzog, Liza. (2007, October). An Early Warning System. *Educational Leadership, 65*(2).

Levin, H. M. (1972). *The cost to the Nation of Inadequate Education*. Select Committee on Equal Educational Opportunity, United States Senate. Ninety-first Congress, Second Session. Washington, D.C.: U.S. Government Printing Office, 3503-3538.

Mourshed, Mona; Chijioke, Chinezi; & Barber, Michael. (2010). *How the World's Most Improved School Systems Keep Getting Better*. McKinsey and Company. www.mckinsey.com

Wilkinson, Richard & Pickett, Kate (2009). *The Spirit Level: Why More Equal Societies Almost Always Do Better*. Allen Lane

ONTARIO HAS PRODUCED A WIDE RANGE OF RESOURCES TO SUPPORT TEACHERS WORKING WITH IMMIGRANT STUDENTS:

Many Roots: Many Voices (www.edu.gov.on.ca)

Supporting English Language Learners with Limited Prior Schooling (www.edu.gov.on.ca)

Supporting English Language Learners: A Practical Guide for Ontario Educators (www.edu.gov.on.ca)

"English Language Learners: ESL and ELD Programs and Services: Policies and Procedures for Ontario's Elementary and Secondary Schools." Ontario Ministry of Education. 2007. www.edu.gov.on.ca,

Cummins. Jim. "Promoting Literacy in Multilingual Contexts." *What Works? Research Into Practice*. Literacy and Numeracy Secretariat. June 2007. (www.edu.gov.on.ca)

"Teaching and Learning in Multicultural Ontario." Literacy and Numeracy Secretariat.www.curriculum.org.

Avis Glaze, on Equity

ACHIEVING EXCELLENCE
WITH EQUITY: A MANDATE
FOR ALL SCHOOLS

School systems across the globe today are focused on improving educational outcomes for their students. Politicians are demanding it, parents and the public are expecting it, and students deserve it. The clarion call for improvement is based on moral, economic, demographic, enlightened self-interest, community health, social justice, global competitiveness, and human rights imperatives. There is a need for all of us as educators to draw upon our rich knowledge base and repertoire of strategies that work to improve our education systems with a sense of urgency.

The cacophony of demands is being heard at a time when school systems are becoming increasingly diverse, with exploding demands and dwindling resources. It is clear that our success and effectiveness will be judged on our ability to provide both excellence and equity in student achievement and wellbeing. Our major challenge, and, indeed our moral responsibility, is to close achievement gaps and to ensure that all students achieve to the maximum of their potential. This is essential not only for individual achievement but also for the future well-being of our society.

In truly equitable systems, factors such as socio-economic status, race, and gender do not truncate students' life chances or prevent them from reaching high levels of achievement. In these systems, educators draw upon their rich repertoire of resources, remove school-based barriers to achievement, and ensure that their schools create the conditions to ensure success. They focus on factors over which we as educators have control: instructional practices, targeted supports for struggling students, strategies to improve student engagement, and positive relationships, which can be very motivating for students. Throughout my 40 years of experience in education, I am always reminded of the power in the statement, obviously attributed to a student: "I don't care how much you know until I know how much you care!"

District and school administrators have the power to influence the day-to-day actions of staff and students. They need to use their influence to instill a sense of urgency within their school systems to raise the bar for all students, to close achievement gaps, and to create the conditions for success for all — especially those who have historically under-performed. Among all the excuses that we make for underperformance, two of their mindset should be that poverty should not determine destiny and that there can be no "throwaway" kids. Our society needs all of our children to be educated so that they can become productive and engaged citizens.

When we look at the highest performing school systems in the world, they are systems that not only strive for excellence but are committed to equity of outcomes:

> Successful schools tend to be those that bolster the performance of students from less advantaged backgrounds. Similarly, countries that have the highest levels of performance tend to be those that are successful in not only raising the learning bar, but also levelling it. (Willms, 2006, p. 67).

In their study of the world's best performing school systems, Barber and Mourshed (2007) found that these systems constantly monitored student progress and constructed interventions to assist individual students in order to prevent them from falling behind — they focused on preventing early failure from compounding into long-term failure. In short, they focused on equity.

While we know that schools can't control the background factors that can impact student achievement, we can control the factors in the school that can help all children achieve their potential. We have to work with our staff to ensure that they recognize the potential in every child. We need to ensure consistent implementation of the instructional strategies that research has shown to be effective in improving achievement for all students.

Our job is to motivate students, teach them effectively, and develop in them a love of learning.

In Ontario's equity and inclusive education strategy, entitled *Realizing the Promise of Diversity* (2009), the Ministry of Education states that an equitable and inclusive education:

- Is a foundation for excellence;

- Meets individual needs;

- Identifies and eliminates barriers;

- Promotes a sense of belonging;

- Involves the broad community;

- Builds on and enhances previous and existing initiatives;

- Is demonstrated throughout the system.

Educators are working to ensure that equity and inclusive education strategies are evident in their programs, policies, practices, and interactions.

High-Impact Strategies to Close Achievement Gaps

A few years ago, we identified 21 high-impact strategies that have been shown to improve student achievement and equity of outcomes. We organized these strategies into five key areas of focus.

- An Inclusive School Culture

- Instructional Practice (using research-informed instructional practices)

- Culturally Responsive Classroom Experiences

- Early Interventions

- Character Development (developing a climate of trust, respect, and community)

As you look at the strategies that we outline, the vast majority of them do not take an inordinate amount of money or additional resources. What they do take is a commitment to change and a willingness to take risks and try different instructional approaches. The research has been clear, for many years, that these strategies work. The problem has been that they have not been implemented consistently in all of our schools, which means that not all of our students have had the same access to these high-impact strategies. The question we have to ask ourselves is, if these strategies have been shown to work, why aren't all schools implementing them in a consistent and intentional manner?

INCLUSIVE SCHOOL CULTURE:

- Establish high expectations for all students

- Build relationships

- Help students feel safe and respected at school

- Offer flexible programming
- Establish career development as an integral part of the curriculum

INSTRUCTIONAL PRACTICES

- Focus on literacy across all subjects
- Develop oral language
- Differentiate instruction
- Emphasize higher order and critical thinking skills
- Make formative assessment integral to learning
- Integrate the arts

CULTURALLY RESPONSIVE CLASSROOM EXPERIENCES

- Practice culturally responsive teaching
- Make classroom activities culturally responsive
- Select culturally reflective learning materials and resources

EARLY INTERVENTIONS

- Implement early and ongoing interventions
- Provide tutoring
- Support summer learning opportunities
- Strengthen access to guidance and counseling

CHARACTER DEVELOPMENT

- Identify character attributes
- Promote inclusive practices

- Maximize student engagement

Would you consider your school/district to be an equitable system? Do your schools/districts:

- Ensure access and inclusion;

- Create positive school and classroom environments based on respect and empathy;

- Build positive relationships among staff, between students and school staff, with parents and the community;

- Use a variety of strategies to close achievement gaps;

- Accommodate diverse learning styles;

- Connect students to real-life and culturally relevant experiences, and

- Involve parents in meaningful ways?

As educators, we have a moral obligation to act as advocates for equity. We need to take on those issues that enhance life circumstances, especially for those people who experience social or economic disadvantage. Our challenge is to work diligently to bring about change that will result in better outcomes for our most vulnerable students.

As advocates for equity, we need to ask ourselves:

- Are we committed to removing barriers to ensure a more just and equitable society?

- Are we willing to confront issues that evoke discomfort and dissonance?

- What will it take to achieve our goals for more equitable and inclusive schools?

We also have a responsibility to speak out publicly about the issues that we face in schools, offering recommendations for improvement. With all the problems that call upon our resources today, and as we compete with health and social services for dwindling resources, educators must continue to be seen be seen as solution finders. Over the years, we have demonstrated our resilience and willingness to work in the most challenging of circumstances.

The most powerful and sustainable change happens from within an organization, not when it is imposed from outside. If we are convinced that the status quo is unacceptable in terms of the achievement of certain groups of students — those who live in poverty, immigrants, racialized groups, Aboriginal students, or students with special education needs, to name a few — then we must use our energy and resources to influence decision making to improve their life chances. Equity work changes the status quo. There is no doubt that there are many barriers to be broken and obstacles to be overcome. It is not an easy path, it requires advo-cacy, hard work, and an unrelenting sense of mission and purpose.

Our experience and the research have show that schools in challenging circumstances can close achievement gaps. Our job as 21st-century educators is to remove all excuses from the table, regain our confidence in our ability to make systems work for the benefit of all students, strengthen our resolve, break the barriers that stand in the way of achieving equity of outcomes for all stu-dents, and recommit ourselves to what we know is possible.

Resources:

Barber, M., &Mourshed, M. (2007). How the world's best-per-forming school systems come out on top. London: McKinsey & Company.

Glaze, Avis; Mattingley, Ruth; and Andrews, Rob. (2013). *High School Graduation: K-12 Strategies that Work*. Corwin. Thousand Oaks. California.

Ontario Ministry of Education (2009). *Realizing the promise of diversity: Ontario's equity and inclusive education strategy*. Toronto: Queen's Printer for Ontario.

Willms, D. (2006). *Learning divides: Ten policy questions about the performance and equity of schools and schooling systems*. (UIS Working Paper No. 5). Montreal, QC: UNESCO Institute for Statistics.

Avis Glaze
(with Ruth Mattingley)
on Literacy

Published in
Reading Forum:NZ. New Zealand Reading Association.
Vol. 27 No. 1, 2012. Pp. 29-35

LITERACY UNLOCKS DOORS...
LITERACY LIBERATES!

**Avis Glaze, President, Edu-quest International Inc., &
Former Chief Student Achievement Officer of Ontario**

**Ruth Mattingley, Former Superintendent of Education, &
Senior Executive Officer, The Literacy and
Numeracy Secretariat**

Our quest for educational equity and excellence must be relentless. Building and developing a robust education system is a challenge we must all embrace. We are called to educate a generation of students that will raise our communities and countries to new heights of attainment. We are not sure what the world that we are preparing our students for will look like. But what we do know is that it will be a much more complex and ever-changing world. It is, therefore, essential that we provide our students with the skills and knowledge necessary to be life-long learners, effective problem-solvers, and critical thinkers. To do that, we must first provide them with a sound foundation in literacy.

Literacy is the key that unlocks the door to future success. It is the most important outcome of schooling — indeed, it affects later educational and social choices. It is the foundation for learning and success in school and helps students secures a better livelihood and makes possible full participation in society. Literacy contributes to one's life chances, sense of personal fulfilment, and employability. Ensuring that students in our schools today are literate is both empowering and liberating.

The first step in improving student achievement for all students is to ensure that they have a sound literacy foundation. In the OECD report, *No More Failures*, Field, Kuczera, and Pont (2007) point out that literacy provides an essential tool for working and living; it is a foundation for nearly all higher-order thinking skills. Research has shown that students who drop out of school often struggle with reading (2008). As Carr-Hill (2008) states:

> Literacy is very important — many would say a human right. A good quality basic education equips pupils with literacy for life and further learning; literate parents are more likely to keep their children healthy and send their children to school; literate people are better able to access other education and employment opportunities; and collectively, literate societies are better geared to meet development challenges. Indeed, the emergence of knowledge societies makes literacy even more critical than in the past. (p. 9)

For these reasons, it is critical that we provide a solid foundation in literacy for all students. Every teacher should be a teacher of literacy. By incorporating literacy across all content areas, educators have the necessary time to build, strengthen, and consolidate student literacy skills. Helping students attain strong literacy skills will facilitate success in all subject areas. When teachers use content from history, science, or other subject areas during language arts, they are able to go deeper into topics and engage students in higher-order thinking. Research has shown that when students have more opportunities to read and discuss content, integrating their literacy skills in a range of subjects, their reading comprehension improves and conceptual knowledge is strengthened.

In highly successful schools and classrooms, teachers set high expectations for their students, providing opportunities for higher-order and critical thinking. Taylor and Collins (2003) point out that successful literacy programs require the presence of educators who believe that literacy can be achieved. When students know that their teachers believe in them, they are more engaged and motivated, resulting in improved student achievement. To strengthen literacy skills, it is important for teachers to differentiate their instruction and provide content that is relevant, addresses student needs and interests, and reflects the diversity of the classroom. A focus on non-fiction writing has also been shown to be an effective strategy to improve student achievement. Douglas Reeves (2002) points out that, "with the exception of attendance, opportunities to develop skills and abilities in non-fiction writing is the 'number-one factor' associated with improved test scores."

Research has shown that elementary schools that provide large uninterrupted blocks of time for the implementation of a balanced literacy program give students a sound literacy foundation. An effective literacy program uses:

- regular read-alouds
- shared reading
- modelled writing
- guided reading and writing
- independent reading and writing

It is important for schools to maintain the focus on literacy throughout high school. Once again, every teacher, regardless of subject specialty, must be a teacher of literacy. As students progress through the grades, they are expected to read increasingly complex material. They need instruction and guidance as they tackle these texts. Students require instruction on how to analyze the features of texts, how to interpret graphic representations, and how to use tables of contents, chapter summaries, and indexes. They need to be able to relate materials they read to prior knowledge and their own experiences. They need opportunities to formulate opinions and summarize material. Teachers of all subjects must provide explicit instruction in their content areas to strengthen student literacy.

If students enter high school with reading skills below grade level, they often give up before they get started. Struggling readers find the texts across subject areas challenging and confusing. To succeed in high school, they need support and ongoing reading instruction. Struggling readers need to believe that they can read and write, and need to experience success in the classroom. As the Ontario Ministry of Education (2003) puts it, they need:

- knowledge of different types of texts and the best strategies for reading them.

- multiple and meaningful opportunities to practise reading in subject-specific contexts.

- opportunities to practise reading with appropriate resources.

- opportunities to talk about their reading and thinking.

- background knowledge in subject areas.

- expanded sight vocabularies and word-solving strategies for reading subject-specific texts.

- strategies for previewing texts, monitoring their understanding, determining the most important ideas and the relationships among them, remembering what they read, and making connections and inferences.

- strategies for becoming independent readers in any context. (p. 7)

In order to build strong literacy skills, students need opportunities to strengthen their oral language. Oral language is the foundation for literacy success. Giving students opportunities for purposeful talk strengthens literacy skills. Some students enter school with a far greater vocabulary than others, which can create gaps at the outset of their educational experience.

> By the time middle-class kids with well-educated parents are in the third grade, they probably know 12,000 words... Meanwhile, kids of undereducated parents who don't talk to them very much probably have vocabularies of 4,000 words by the time they are in third grade—a third as many words as their middle-class peers. That's why it's important to start early on with vocabulary development, because you bring disadvantaged children much closer to the developmental trajectory of the students from highly educated, middle-class families. That is the mechanism for shrinking the achievement gap. (Snow, 2005)

This observation has been substantiated by Germeroth, Barker, Arens, and Wang (2009). They point out that by Kindergarten, the difference in numbers of words heard between children of low and high socio-economic status could be as many as 32 million words over the course of a year. Providing students with opportunities to build their vocabulary and use it in meaningful ways will help reduce achievement gaps.

Time for purposeful talk and interaction is necessary for real learning to occur. Teachers should provide time for students to share ideas, develop their opinions, debate, and clarify their thinking prior to writing. These tasks enable students to learn to respect the opinions of others, build upon ideas of the group, and consolidate their thinking.

Improving Boys' Literacy

Not so long ago, most gender differences in school outcomes favoured boys. The situation, however, has changed dramatically in the last few decades. Now, across the world, girls are outperforming boys in literacy achievement both in elementary schools and in secondary schools. "Girls have been shown to have a significant and consistent advantage from an early age over boys, and this advantage is found not only in North America and English-speaking countries, but internationally across cultures and languages" (Klinger et al., 2009).

A challenge in thinking about gender issues is the risk of treating boys or girls as homogeneous groups who all like similar things or require similar strategies. In fact, the differences among boys or among girls are much greater than the differences between the two groups. It is important to be aware of research findings on educating boys and girls, but not to assume that one size fits each gender.

SPECIFIC STRATEGIES FOR BOYS

Schools often perpetuate the status quo by assuming that "boys will be boys," and that they are not interested in reading and writing. Preconceived notions that boys will not meet with success in reading and writing and not enjoy school need to be eradicated. We cannot lower expectations based on our assumptions about boys. Myhill and Jones (2006) point out that even at a very young age, students understand that teachers treat boys and girls differently.

The 2009 PISA (Programme for International Student Assessment) report states that:

> Since most of the gender gap can be explained by boys being less engaged, and less engaged students show lower performance, then policy makers should look for more effective ways of increasing boys' interest in reading at school or at home. (OECD, 2010, p. 12)

Believing that boys can achieve in literacy at high levels, differentiating our approach and engaging them in relevant learning experiences can make a difference. Sound pedagogy in a caring and responsive environment will reap great rewards for our students. If boys feel valued by their teachers, then they will be motivated to learn. If they feel supported, they will feel safe to take chances. The often-used slogan, "engage me or enrage me," could become the clarion call for boys who do not see the relevance of classroom content or are not achieving the success of which they are capable.

To improve boys' achievement in literacy, teachers need to differentiate their instructional practices. In the research paper "Boys' Literacy Attainment," Booth et al. (2009) point out that when addressing the needs of boys, educators need to use context-appropriate curriculum and research-based instructional practice, and not be taken in by "Band-Aid" innovations that group boys into one homogeneous mass. They go on to say that grouping and educating boys as if they were a homogenous category does them a serious injustice. For example, not all boys are failing standardized tests, doing less well than girls, or hate to read. It is, therefore, important, just as it is with all students, to disaggregate achievement data to determine which boys are struggling and in which specific areas. Not all boys are interested in the same things, and they do not all learn in the same manner.

An international study of effective teaching strategies was conducted by Reichert and Hawley (2009). They found that when they asked teachers to share instructional strategies that were especially helpful in reaching boys, there were profound similarities in their practice. Nearly every lesson included multiple elements that took into account differing learning styles, interests, and abilities. The researchers grouped the instructional strategies into categories, which included:

- gaming,
- motor activities,
- role play and drama,
- open inquiry,
- teamwork and competition,
- personal realization,
- responsibility for outcomes,
- intrinsic subject matter, and
- novelty and surprise.

Reichert and Hawley also asked male students, aged 12 to 19, to share their thoughts about effective teaching. The teacher qualities that the boys said contributed to their learning included:

- light-heartedness and good humour,
- patience, and
- belief in their students' abilities.

It is evident from the student responses that building positive relationships is an essential component of an effective learning environment for boys. While positive relationships with teachers have value for all students, they particularly work for boys.

Students are a valuable resource in selecting materials for the classroom or library. By being consulted, they develop a sense of ownership and interest in the new resources. Ask students what they like to read and have them help select books or bring in books from home to share. Ensuring that classroom libraries have a wide variety of reading materials is critical to encouraging boys to read.

At times, our lesson plans and the way we respond to students have more to do with our own interests, learning styles, and experiences than those of our students. Our personal likes and dislikes can affect how we plan the learning environment for our students. Without realizing it, we have organized instruction that misses the mark when it comes to engaging our students. As Fletcher (2006) points out, "It is important for us to become aware of our own subjective tastes and broaden our repertoire if we are going to engage boys in literacy" (p. 24).

In *The Road Ahead: Boys' Literacy Teacher Inquiry Project* (OISE, 2009), teachers state that some boys do not believe they are reading if they are not reading classroom text-type materials or full-length novels. This belief impacted their attitudes and feelings that they were not good readers. Teachers should know and teach a variety of traditional and non-traditional genres. The reading that boys do should not be dismissed as inconsequential, even though it may not include the novels and other traditional materials found in most classrooms.

Teachers need to acknowledge the value of the wide range of writing that students do in their daily lives and provide classroom opportunities for such writing. Boys are more engaged when the work seems relevant to them, in other words, when it has a purpose they can understand. Many boys who do not like to read and write at school are choosing to sit at their computer and read and write for hours when at home. They text their friends, write about their strategies when gaming, and share their thoughts and feelings through e-mails. Their writing has become a social activity facilitated by such venues as e-mail and Facebook. We might not like the spelling or the vocabulary, but they are reading and writing.

A sign of the changing times is that the *Oxford English Dictionary*, in the March 2011 revision, recognized language being used on social networks such as "LOL" (laugh out loud) as an acceptable means of communication. Our classrooms could make good use of the language and communication techniques used by our students. The question to educators is how can we take that passion and enthusiasm boys show for this form of communication and bring it into the classroom? Too often, our classrooms do not recognize student preferences as having academic value.

Most students, and especially boys, enjoy using technology. Making technology an integral part of the classroom experience will help engage boys in reading and writing. The Internet and other multimedia resources can be an effective catalyst for students to think, analyze and discuss. Technology can expand students' learning beyond the classroom walls. It provides real world issues and relevant topics. When boys engage in literacy for authentic reasons and have opportunities through inquiry to investigate, analyze, problem-solve, and formulate opinions, they gain a deeper appreciation for reading and writing as practical and necessary life skills.

Students take more ownership and feel more independent when they have choice in their assignments. "Boys who were allowed to exercise some choice around their reading selections and writing topics showed increased motivation and engagement" (Me Read? And How!, p. 10). Most students take ownership for their learning when they are taught effective negotiating skills and allowed choice within reasonable limits. Teachers can address different learning styles more effectively when students are given choice.

Oral language is the foundation for literacy development. Many boys need to talk through their ideas before they are sure they understand what they have read or before they can put pen to paper. Encouraging purposeful talk is critical to helping students build on one another's ideas and consolidate thinking. In an effective classroom, "talk is the hidden glue that cements students' understandings while simultaneously bringing together the classroom community" (Fletcher, 2006, p. 81). Too often, we give students a topic and immediately ask them to put pencil to paper.

Students need time to consolidate their thinking. Purposeful talk allows them to do so before they write.

It is necessary for teachers to be cognizant of who is talking in their classrooms. Do all students have an equal opportunity to share their ideas? Who are the students that are called upon the most to contribute to class discussions? Teachers need to provide opportunities for students in general and boys in particular to share their ideas, discuss their opinions, defend their position, and challenge the content they have read. They want to be actively engaged. Like all students, boys require time for review and reflection. Boys need time to talk, reflect, to think deeply, explore the views of others, and question one another's thinking in a respectful way. Their achievement will also improve when they are given timely and precise feedback with encouragement and support.

Summary

Our classrooms are a microcosm of the larger society. The students in our classrooms have a range of interests, abilities, experiences, traditions, and knowledge. As educators, it is our moral responsibility to reach out to each and every one of these students and provide them with an education that meets their needs and helps them to achieve to high levels. We need to build the capacity of our schools so they deliver on the promise of a literacy guarantee.

It is critical for all students to develop strong literacy skills if they are going to be successful in this knowledge-based, information-rich economy if they are to develop 21st-century skills. Research has clearly shown that early school achievement, especially in reading and writing is one of the greatest predictors of future success. We need to ensure that we are helping all students achieve, by giving them a sound foundation in literacy. Our students will need high levels of literacy to be contributing, thriving members of society. High levels of literacy will empower them and provide the skills they need to function effectively as contributing and engaged members of society. Literacy is the master key to future learning and career opportunities. Literacy liberates.

References

Booth, D.; Elliott-Johns, S.; & Bruce, F. (2009). *Boys' Literacy Attainment: Research and Related Practice.* A report prepared for the Ontario Ministry of Education. Retrieved from www.edu. gov.on.ca/eng/research/boys_literacy.pdf

Carbo, R. (2008). *Strategies for Increasing Achievement in Reading.* In R.W. Cole (Ed.), Educating Everybody's Children: Diverse Teaching Strategies for Diverse Learners. (pp. 98-122). Alexandria, VA: ASCD.

Carr-Hill, R. (2008). *International Literacy Statistics: A Review of Concepts, Methodology and Current Data.* Montreal, PQ: UNESCO Institute for Statistics. Retrieved from http://uis. unesco.org/template/pdf/Literacy/LiteracyReport 2008.pdf

Field, S.; Kuczera, M.; & Pont, B. (2007). No More Failures: *Ten Steps to Equality in Education.* Paris, France. OECD.

Fletcher, R. (2006). *Boy Writers: Reclaiming Their Voices.* Markham, ON: Pembroke Publishers.

Germeroth, C.; Barker, J; Arens, S.; & Wang, X. (2009, October 30). *Our Kids.* (A McREL report prepared for the Stupski Foundation's Learning System). Denver, CO; McREL.

Glaze, Avis; Mattingley, Ruth & Levin, Ben. (2012). Breaking Barriers: Excellence and Equity for All. Pearson Canada Inc. Toronto, Canada. 2012.

Klinger, D.; Shulha, L.A.; & Wade-Woolley, L. (2009) *Towards an Understanding of Gender Differences in Literacy Achievement.* (A study prepared for the Education and Accountability Office.) Retrieved from www.eqao.com

Myhill, D.; & Jones, S. (2006). *She Doesn't Shout at No Girls: Pupils Perceptions of Gender Equity in the Classroom.* Cambridge Journal of Education, 36(1).

OECD. (2010). *PISA 2009 Results: Learning to Learn — Student Engagement, Strategies and Practices*. (Vol. 3). Paris, France, OECD.

Ontario Ministry of Education. (2009). *Me Read? And How? Ontario Teachers Report on How to Improve boys' literacy skills*. Toronto, ON: Queen's Printer. Retrieved from www.edu.gov.on.ca/eng/curriculum/meRead_andHow.pdf

Ontario Ministry of Education. (2003). *Think Literacy: Cross-Curricular Approaches Grades 7-12*. Retrieved from http://www.edu.gov.on.ca/eng/studentsuccess/thinkliteracy/

Reeves, D. (2002, March/ April). *Harvard Education Letter*.

Reichert, M.; & Hawley, R. (2009). *Reaching Boys: An International Study of Effective Teaching*. Phi Delta Kappan, 91(4), 35-40.

Snow, C. (2005, July/August). *From Literacy to Learning*. Harvard Education Letter.

Taylor, R.; & Collins, V.D. (2003). Literacy for Leadership for Grades 5-12. Alexandria, VA: ASCD.

The Road Ahead: Boys' Literacy Teacher Inquiry Project. (2009). OISE, University of Toronto.

Avis Glaze
(with Ouida M. Wright)
on Improving the Educational
and Life Chances of
African Canadian Youth

IMPROVING THE EDUCATIONAL AND LIFE CHANCES OF AFRICAN CANADIAN YOUTH: INSIGHTS FROM ONTARIO'S ROYAL COMMISSION ON LEARNING

Avis E. Glaze, Ed.D.
Ouida M. Wright, Ph.D., F.C.C.T

The system of education in Ontario, despite its faults, is recognized as one of the best in the world. There are many pockets of excellence and some areas that need improvement. It has, however, become imperative that the education system, as a major change agent in our society, re-evaluate its role and effectiveness in responding to its increasingly diverse population and to the rapidly mutating needs of the individuals we are expected to serve.

The urgency for change and improvement is driven by many factors: the worldwide emphasis on the need for higher standards and greater accountability; the increased emphasis on excellence in student achievement and on their engagement in the learning process; the emphasis on educating all children to a much higher level; the rapid developments in science and technology and their application in every field of endeavour; and, the competitiveness of the global marketplace and the dwindling natural and economic resources.

We do know that, historically, when resources dwindle, cries for accountability intensify. The flurry of activity in most countries over the last ten years to restructure and reform education is a testimony to the fact that there is widespread recognition that change, resulting from public discontent, is expected. Parents and students want more meaningful participation in the educational process, the general public wants more value for every dollar spent on education, and parents from ethno-racial communities want greater success for their children within the educational system.

A. The Commission

1. THE COMMISSION'S MANDATE

In May, 1993, in response to continuing concerns about the quality, economy, and responsiveness of the system of education in Ontario, the Ontario Minister of Education established a **Royal Commission on Learning**, which was charged with the responsibility to bring all partners in the educational system together in a process of public consultation and to take the public's concerns and translate them into a concrete plan of action for the future of the elementary and secondary school education in Ontario. The Commission's mandate, which was developed in consultation at six public forums across Ontario and with a working group of stakeholders, posed several questions under the following themes: the purpose and direction of our school system; the program in our schools; accountability in education; and, the organization of our system and the issue of governance.

The Commission's mandate dictated that the Constitution and Charter Rights of Roman Catholics and Francophones should be respected in any consideration to modify governance structures, and that the needs of native students being educated off reserves and the impact of provincial policies of education on reserves should be addressed. It must be noted that the governance of education of on-reserve aboriginal peoples is a self-governance issue — one that would be addressed through separate processes.

2. THE CONSULTATION

Public consultation was extensive. It included information book-lets, advertisements in local newspapers, twelve weeks of public hearings in 27 cities throughout the province, radio, television, and newspaper interviews and an education "summit" produced by TV Ontario. The Commission arranged for research papers, spoke to experts, and visited schools. In an effort to reach those who might not respond to these more formal processes, the Commission also visited such places as shopping malls, community centres, newly arrived immigrant groups, and specific cultural organizations, detention centres, and homes for pregnant teens.

The Commission also spoke with the authors who were avail-able and reviewed a range of reports on education that had been commissioned by the Government of Ontario over the previous 18 years. These include The Hall/Dennis Report (1968) on the aims and objectives of education in Ontario, **The Radwanski Report** (1987) on educational relevance and the drop-out rate, and **The Stephen Lewis Report** (1992), which offered advice on race relations and racism in the educational system. (A list of some of the previous reports on education that we reviewed is provided in Appendix 1. This is by no means an exhaustive list of relevant reports).

Common themes were evident in past reports. There were concerns about accountability and standards, testing and student achievement; the need for equity; partnerships and linkages; improved programs for young children, for adolescents, and for students with special needs; lifelong learning; program relevance, flexibility, clarity, and coherence; and, the need to reduce the drop-out rate. The following observation from The Hall/Dennis Report is as relevant today as it was then:

> Today, on every side, however, there is heard a growing demand for a fresh look at education in Ontario. The Committee was told of inflexible programs, outdated

curricula, unrealistic regulations, regimented organization, and mistaken aims of education. We heard from
alienated students, frustrated teachers, irate parents and
concerned educators. Many public organizations and
private individuals have told us of their growing discontent and lack of confidence in a system, which, in their
opinion, has become outmoded and is failing those it
exists to serve. (The Hall/Dennis Report, page 10.)

As a result of this very extensive consultation with the widest
possible cross-section of Ontarians, the Commissioners of the
Royal Commission on Learning concluded that Ontario does have
a good educational system with some excellent schools and many
committed educators. They did, however, state that there are
many aspects of the system that require dramatic improvement if
the system is to enhance the opportunities and life chances of students, in general, and of those from racial minorities and homes
with low incomes, in particular.

3. THE REPORT

The Commission presented its Report in January 1995, within a
political, economic, demographic, and social context that reflected
the increasing turbulence in society at that time. The picture we
would paint of that context was one in which there was: increased
politicization of education; the rise of the "back to the basics"
movement; the continuing recession; globalization and competition for dwindling economic resources; increasing diversity in the
demography of the province; the revolutionalization of education by information technology and the movement towards the
Communication Age; demands for equity based on race, gender,
socio-economic status, and sexual orientation; the rise of the powerful equity backlash; the emergence of a students as a political
sub-culture; the return of many adults to formal education; and,
the elusiveness of obtaining consensus on any issue. The Report

was released as four printed volumes, a Short Version in a single volume, as well as a CD-ROM version. The Report received the support of all parties in the Legislature as well as enthusiastic media and public response.

After examining some 5,000 briefs, the Commissioners concluded that the conventional tools of school reform are just not enough to transform Ontario's massive educational system in the many ways in which we considered necessary. We redefined the primary and shared responsibilities of schools with a clear focus on schools as centres of teaching and learning. We advanced a two-tiered system of recommendations, and identified four engines or levers of change:

a. **The first engine: A new kind of school-community alliance**

Within the report of the Royal Commission on Learning, the commonly-used African saying, "It takes a whole village to raise a child," reflected our thinking as we discussed the importance of bringing together the many groups and services necessary to support learning. These resources — parents, community organizations, social agencies, business and unions, religious, cultural and athletic groups — must play their parts. In this regard, the Commissioners recommended that every school establish a school-community council with staff, students, parents, and community representatives to create links between the school and the community and to provide advice on key issues.

At the provincial level, it was recommended that a senior minister be responsible for the coordination of services to children and to facilitate collaboration among the other government agencies responsible for the welfare of children. Another reason for the emphasis on Community Education is the fact that many teachers told us they are overburdened with an overcrowded curriculum and that they were not able to focus on their primary role — that of enhancing the intellectual competence of students. Our conclusion was that schools cannot do it alone. They need assistance with the shared aspects of education so that they can focus their attention on the academic achievement of students.

b. **The second engine: Early childhood education**

The Commission was indeed impressed with the body of research that points to the benefits that accrue not only to individuals but to society as a whole as a result of high-quality early childhood education programs. Early learning has a tremendous impact on future success in school. Children who experience high-quality programs not only gain significantly in coping skills but also develop positive attitudes to learning. A secure, supportive learning environment at an early age is also a way of making sure all students have the same opportunities and that learning problems are identified and remediated early.

c. **The third engine: The professionalization of teachers**

The Commissioners recognize fully that no real reform can take place without the participation of teachers. They must be given the support that they need to fulfil their increasingly challenging role. Professionals learn throughout their lives. They are expected to engage in ongoing professional development to ensure continuous improvement. We recommended that professional development be mandatory for all educators and that an Ontario College of Teachers be established as an independent body to determine professional standards and be responsible for certifying teachers. The College would also accredit teacher education programs. As well, we recommended that teacher preparation programs be extended to two years with a substantial portion of the second year being devoted to practical experience in schools with exemplary teachers.

d. **The fourth engine: Information technology**

As Commissioners, we recognized that information technology offers boundless promise in a world where computer literacy is becoming as essential as print literacy. Information technology has the potential to radically transform the nature of teaching and learning. Through computers, students can learn problem-solving skills as well as higher order analytic and critical thinking skills. It also provides them with access to a whole new world of information beyond the walls of the school. We encourage business and government to provide schools with the network links, appropriate technological resources, and professional development that teachers need in order to fulfil the true promise of information technology in educational settings.

In support of these four engines, there are 167 recommendations in a variety of areas. They address the many challenges facing education in Ontario. The Commissioners were confident that solutions regarding educational quality, equity, partnerships and accountability are ensured in these recommendations. The school, curriculum, students, teachers, and society-at-large will benefit. If implemented, Ontarians would be in a better position to meet the educational challenges of the 21st century with confidence.

4. ONTARIO'S DIVERSE COMMUNITIES

The Commission was impressed with the "astonishing diversity that characterizes the people of Ontario" (Short Version, page 43). Indeed, a wide range of religious, linguistic, racial, and ethnocultural groups seized on the opportunity to air their concerns about the education of their children. It was clear to the Commission "that schools must welcome students of every background, faith, language, culture, or colour. On this there can be no compromise or qualification." (Short Version, page 43). In particular, representatives of the various racial and ethnocultural groups and organizations submitted briefs, often including irrefutable empirical data such as abnormally high drop-out rates and the number going into university, which demonstrated "forcefully and convincingly that the educational system was failing their community" (Short Version, page 44). This was particularly true for the Black, Hispanic/Latin, and Portuguese communities, as well as Francophone and Aboriginal groups and organizations. Indeed, their comments were echoed by Stephen Lewis in his report on race relations in 1992:

> ...it's as if virtually nothing has changed for visible minority kids in the school system over the last ten years. The lack of real progress is shocking. And I believe it signals the most intractable dilemma, around race relations, in contemporary education: How do you get the best of policies and programs into the individual classrooms? It raises searching questions of communications..." (Stephen Lewis Report, page 20)

Among its many recommendations, the Lewis report asked that the Ministry monitor the implementation of employment equity in schools and in the Ministry itself, and that faculties of education review their admissions criteria to attract and enrol more qualified members of minority groups.

5. THE CONCERNS AND PROPOSALS OF THE AFRICAN-CANADIAN COMMUNITY

Many concerns were expressed by parents and community leaders within the African community. The methods offered for addressing them reflected strategies that community members have proposed over the years in many different forums. Educators and community leaders from organizations such as the Organization for the Parents of Black Children (OPBC), the Black Educators' Working Group (BEWG), and the Anti-racist Multicultural Educators' Network of Ontario (AMENO), who have worked long and hard with school boards and the Ministry of Education and Training in support of more effective education for black and other racial minority students, asserted that black children are casualties of negative differential treatment, stereotyping, bias in testing and evaluation, streaming, a monocultural curriculum, unfair and unusual discipline, racism, and most damaging of all, the self-fulfilling prophecy of low expectations. Many of the concerns, some of which were shared by other ethnocultural groups and organizations, were voiced with a sense of urgency and underscoring the notion that there was a crisis in the African-Canadian community in terms of the education of their students. Some of the concerns were expressed as follows:

a. A disproportionate number of students are dropping out, failing, or being streamed into low academic levels or special education classes. The system is clearly not utilizing the potential of these students.

b. The curriculum is not inclusive. Students do not see themselves reflected in the curriculum — their literature, history, or the achievements of their community — and when mention is made, it is often in a negative or stereotypic manner.

c. Some teachers have low expectations of black students and expect them to fail or do poorly.

d. Strong biases still exist in psychological tests and do not take into account differences in educational, cultural, and social backgrounds.

e. Black students have few role models in the school system, and teachers trained in other countries have little access to the teaching profession.

f. Stereotyping and racism are "rampant" in the school system.

g. Too many students of African heritage are directed towards athletics and "choice-limiting" programs as a first option.

h. Police officers are called to deal with black students for even minor incidents. Often the victim, in defending himself or herself from verbal or physical assault, becomes the offender.

In short, the briefs suggest that many black students feel alienated from and marginalized within the education system. The briefs made a number of suggestions and recommendations, including the following:

The present curriculum puts very little emphasis on minority cultures and contributions. An inclusive curriculum, including Black Studies, is necessary for all schools and not just for those with populations of African-Canadian and other racial and ethno-cultural minorities. When International Languages are offered at the elementary level, Black Studies should also be offered.

a. More minority teachers must be hired to reflect the racial and cultural backgrounds of Ontario schools.

b. Schools and school boards should be more accountable for performance and results, and there should be better reporting of student achievement.

c. Parents should be more actively involved in the education of their children, e.g. there should be an Advisory Council and liaison persons to better involve and inform communities and parents. Parents should have meaningful input into policy decisions and be made to feel welcome as part of the life and decision-making within the school.

d. There should be Ombudsperson in each community to deal with minority concerns.

e. There should be mentorship programs for students, better guidance and counselling, and all students should be advised of post-secondary options. Students should not be channelled into occupational fields based on racial or gender stereotypes.

f. Teachers should be trained to identify and eliminate stereotyping and racism, to work with students from a wide range of backgrounds and be knowledgeable about Ontario's rich, diverse multicultural heritage.

g. There should be a better balance between teacher-directed instruction and child-centred learning.

6. THE COMMISSION'S RECOMMENDATION ON RACIAL AND ETHNOCULTURAL EQUITY

Throughout the Report, the Commissioners made a wide range of observations and recommendations that touch upon the needs and concerns of religious, language, and ethnic minorities, Aboriginals, Francophones, and Roman Catholics. They recognized and valued the diversity in Canadian society. In their report, they addressed the rights and needs of Roman Catholics, Francophones, and First Nations people, and of religious, language, and ethnic minorities. In relation to Catholic schools, which educate 30% of Ontario students, the Commission recommended that they be better represented in the Ministry of Education and Training, maintain preferential hiring of teachers, and be better served by faculties of education in the preparation of their teachers. The French-language community, also with constitutionally guaranteed rights, is to be given the full governance already decided by the courts.

Regarding First Nations people, the Commission supported ongoing negotiations for the governance of their schools.

The recommendation also supports anti-racism initiatives already introduced by the Ministry of Education and Training to ensure that teaching materials, practices, programs, and assessment tools are free of racism. As well, the flexibility for local communities to design 10% of the curriculum can be used to address the needs of students from various ethnocultural communities. Ninety percent of the curriculum should be developed and provided for the schools of the province by the Ministry of Education and Training.

The following recommendations seem particularly pertinent:

> Recommendation 61: That faculties expand their efforts to admit more student teachers from previously under-represented groups, including ethnocultural and racial minorities, aboriginal communities, and those who are disabled, and that they be accountable to the College of Teachers for demonstrating significant progress towards this objective.

> Recommendation 62: That faculties of education, school boards, and teachers' federations develop joint programs to encourage more young people from minority groups to consider teaching as a career, and to ensure that minority youth and adults interested in teaching have opportunities to gain the necessary experience with children and adolescents.

> Recommendation 104: That school boards, in cooperation with government ministries and appropriate agencies, establish in neighbourhoods where personal computer access is less likely to be prevalent, community computing centres, possibly in school buildings or in public libraries,

and provide on-going funding for hardware, software, and staffing.

Recommendation 108: That the Ministry of Education and Training mandate that each school in Ontario establish a school-community council, with membership drawn from the following sectors:

- parents

- students (from Grade 7 on)

- teachers

- representatives from local religious and ethnic communities

- service providers (government and non-government)

- municipal government(s)

- service clubs and organizations

- business sector.

Recommendation 136: That the Ministry of Education and Training always have an Assistant Deputy Minister responsible, in addition to other duties, for advocacy on behalf of Anglophone, Francophone, ethnocultural, and racial minorities.

Recommendation 137: That trustees, educators, and support staff be provided with professional development in anti-racism.

Recommendation 138: That the performance management process for supervisory officers, principals, and teachers specifically include measurable outcomes related to anti-racism policies and plans of the Ministry and school boards.

Recommendation 139: That, for the purposes of the anti-racism and ethnocultural equity provisions of Bill 21, the Ministry of Education and Training require boards and schools to seek input from parents and community members in implementing and monitoring the plans. This process should be linked to the overall school and board accountability mechanism.

Recommendation 140: That the Ministry and school boards systemically review and monitor teaching materials of all types, reading materials, videos, software, etc., as well as teaching practices, educational programs (curriculum), and assessment tools to ensure that they are free of racism and meet the spirit and letter of anti-racism policies.

Recommendation 141: That in jurisdictions with large numbers of black students, school boards, academic authorities, faculties of education, and representatives of the black community collaborate to establish demonstration schools and innovative programs based on best practices in bringing about academic success for black students.

Recommendation 142: That whenever there are indications of collective underachievement in any particular group of students, school boards ensure that teachers and principals have the necessary strategies and human and financial resources to help these students.

It is evident that the Commission took the concerns into consideration. These recommendations, if implemented, should go a far way to meeting the concerns of a wide range of communities.

B. Improving the Educational and Life Chances of Black Youth

1. THE BLACK COMMUNITY VALUES EDUCATION

Contrary to prevailing mythology, the African-Canadian community has always placed a high value on education. This was demonstrated by the range and quality of the briefs submitted to the Commission, the discussions in the consultative process, and visits to schools. Those who are more recently from the Caribbean, Africa, and other parts of the African diaspora know that, like women in Canadian society, they must work very hard to achieve their goals. But, in their homelands, role models of academic and professional excellence were in abundance. Yet somehow, even for those black students who are descendants of earlier settlers in Ontario, academic excellence is perceived to be the exception rather than the rule.

The myth that black people do not value education, that they cannot, in general, achieve academic excellence, and that parents are not interested in their children's education must be dislodged. Black parents, educators, and organizations have not stood idly by waiting for someone else to address their concerns about their children's education. They have cooperated with school boards and the Ministry of Education and Training in the cause of their children's academic achievement. Indeed, it was the persistent lobbying of the Black Educators' Working Group and The Anti-Racist and Multicultural Educators' Network of Ontario that resulted in the establishment of the position of Assistant Deputy Minister of Anti-Racism and Equity. These two organizations, as well as others, have worked very closely with the Ministry to help define policy.

2. SCHOOL BOARDS AND THE MINISTRY
OF EDUCATION AND TRAINING

The Commission was made aware that some school boards across the province, but particularly where there is a markedly diverse population, have attempted in a variety of ways to respond to the concerns of racial and ethnocultural minorities. Some schools boards in such centres as Metropolitan Toronto, Ottawa, Windsor, and neighbouring regions are successfully implementing innovative programs and working closely with Faculties of Education to address the concerns within the environment of shrinking financial resources. Consultative staff have been hired, curricula developed, in-service training for teachers has been provided; parents have been consulted. For example, the Toronto Board of Education worked with the Organization of Parents of Black Children on The Consultative Committee on the Education of Black Students to produce a landmark report that is currently being implemented. These school boards are to be congratulated and encouraged in this work. Yet much remains to be done, especially in Boards with fairly homogeneous populations. We must convince all educators that all children in Ontario need anti-racist education. This is essential for equity and harmonious relations in an increasingly diverse province, country, and indeed, world.

Over the years, the Ontario Ministry of Education and Training has sought ways to address the communities' concerns. For example, in 1980, in an effort to eliminate racism and stereotyping the Ministry published, *Race, Religion and Culture: Suggestions for Authors and Publishers* to help ensure that textbooks would be free of bias. In 1992, the Government passed Bill 21 and approved Memorandum 119, which required school boards to develop and implement plans to combat racism and provided for guidelines to assist in the implementation. In 1993, the Ministry set up a Division of Anti-Racism, Access and Equity headed by an Assistant Deputy Minister, supported by legislation, staff and financial resources, to eliminate racism and promote equity in the educational system of Ontario. While, with varying degrees of support from school boards, colleges, universities, and communities, this Division has made some significant impact, the initiative has, in recent months, been in danger of being scaled back as the civil service is downsized.

Unfortunately, the division has now been reduced and renamed the Anti-discrimination and Equal Opportunity Branch. Black parents and community organizations are not unaware of the need for economy in the public service and appreciate that the provincial government continues to place some emphasis on issues of equity. Nevertheless, this reduction is discouraging particularly since the *Ontario Secondary Schools* (1998) *Detailed Discussion Document*, which deals with secondary reform in its section on "Antidiscrimination Education," makes no reference to racism or other deeply entrenched prejudices or the role of the school in eliminating them.

3. OTHER GROUPS AND ORGANIZATIONS

Other groups have also seized the initiative. The Black Business and Professional Association annually does fundraising to support the Harry Jerome Awards and provides scholarships for achieving students. Over the last 10 years, there has been a steady increase in the academic averages of applicants for the Harry Gairey scholarships. The John Brooks Foundation Annual Awards continue to identify black students of significant ability and achievement. The Beverley Mascoll Foundation has recently been established to provide financial support to assist young Black people to achieve. Young people are working with indefatigable zeal to achieve excellence in every walk of life.

One of the most noticeable initiatives in this drive has been the Saturday Morning Schools established by groups such as The African Heritage Educators' Network of the (AHEN), a group of North York educators, and the Canadian Alliance of Black Educators (CABE). At these sessions, run by black educators, parents, and other volunteers, young people are coached, mentored and nurtured in an environment that is reflective of their culture and supported by dedicated role models. Their success and some research have been given rise to the idea that black focused schools within the public school system might be a viable alternative and serve as a transition to the more formal secondary education program. This was supported by *Towards a New Beginning: The Four Level Government/African Community Working Group Report* (1992). There are pros and cons to this proposal, but the Four Level Report, the Stephen Lewis Report, as well as the Royal Commission's recommendations, signalled the urgent need for governments, school boards, parents, educators, and communities to intensify efforts to address the issue of the education of black students.

4. CAREER EDUCATION

Career education is an educational equity imperative (Glaze 1993). As an aspect of general education, it has the potential to enhance the roles and the life chances of students. As an instructional strategy, career education has the potential to improve educational outcomes. The activities must be gradual and cumulative, beginning in early childhood, when students learn about the many work roles in their neighbourhoods and the interconnectedness of workers in society to the point at which they begin to explore career alternatives and ultimately make career choices. Career education extends the academic world into the reality of the world of work.

The roles that individuals play in their lives are many and varied. They are students, workers, consumers, citizens, and parents, to name a few. The fulfilment of these life roles and their life chances are dependent on education, generally, and career education, specifically. Career education can help shape their prospects of leading productive, self-sustaining, and satisfying lives. It can rekindle their spirit and instill in them a sense of hope in the future. It has motivated some students to dream and visualize their role and a place in society. Through increased self-awareness, they can also recognize that they have the potential to develop the skills necessary to realize their dreams. Ultimately, everyone benefits — the individuals and society as a whole. If, however, career education is to receive the attention it deserves within the school curriculum, it must not only be seen as an equity imperative; it must become an educational leadership imperative (Glaze 1994).

5. THE ROLE OF TEACHERS AND ADMINISTRATORS

While there is a clear responsibility for parents, it is the schools in which education takes place that are the primary change agents in the educational process. Peter Drucker (1993), says that knowledge will be the primary resource in post-capitalist society. He insists that the basic economic resource or "the means of production," to use the economists' term, is no longer capital, nor natural resource nor labour — it is, and will be knowledge. The leading social groups in society will be "knowledge workers." The knowledge society must have a clear notion of what it means to be educated. He concludes by saying that the educated person will be society's emblem, symbol, and standard bearer. The educated person will be society's archetype.

Drucker also states that the educated person of the future will need more than the traditional notion of the "basics," but will need skills in technology, foreign languages, and skills to be effective members or organizations as employees.

On the question of who is accountable for results as related to student achievement, it is Peter Drucker's view that the school is. In fact, he states his perspective quite bluntly:

> ...we will no longer accept the school teacher's age-old excuse for malpractice: "the students are lazy and stupid."
> With knowledge the central resource in society, lazy

students and poor students are the responsibility of the school. There are then only schools that perform and schools that do not. (Drucker, 1993, p. 208)

Teachers and administrators must also have a clear understanding of what constitutes a truly equitable school. Here are a few key characteristics:

a. Curriculum materials are reviewed consistently for biases such as those related to race, gender, socio-economic status.

b. Materials, including history and literature books, are selected for inclusiveness.

c. The curriculum is user-friendly and does not exclude or alienate students.

d. The staff is reflective of the larger community.

e. The staff is able to recognize and deal with prejudice in self and in students.

f. The staff addresses systemic barriers that limit the life chances of students.

g. The teaching and classroom practices are free of bias.

h. Achievement data are disaggregated by race, gender, socio-economic status.

i. High expectations for achievement are communicated to students.

j. Students see themselves and their cultural backgrounds reflected in the curriculum.

k. Zero-tolerance for racism is clearly articulated.

l. Parents feel welcome in the school and are encouraged to play a meaningful role in their children's education.

m. Cultural and class biases in standardized tests are recognized, and they are not used as a basis for decision-making
around program selection placement of students.

n. To an outsider, placement in programs and learning
groups would not appear to be based on race, gender, or
social class.

o. Students are demitted regularly from special education programs.

p. The culture and management of the school are bias-free.

q. Discipline is applied consistently and fairly.

r. Those who graduate from the school reflect the race,
gender, and socio-economic diversity that exists in
the school.

As teachers and administrators, we must continue to
reflect upon our work and question regularly our basic beliefs
and practices:

- Are we convinced that all students can learn and succeed? If
not, why not?

- Are we preparing all students to see themselves as individuals capable of transforming our world and making the best
use of our shrinking resources?

- Do we work to eliminate stereotyping, individual and systemic racism in the educational environment, and identify
and eradicate systemic barriers and inequities which limit
the life chance of students?

- Do we involve all parents meaningfully in the education of
their children, welcome them as partners into the schools,
and treat them with respect?

- In short, do we as educators see schools as dynamic change agents or are they merely instruments to preserve the status quo? Are we there for all our students or only some of them?

C. Secondary Education Reform
(September 1996)

There is no doubt that we welcome the reform of secondary education in Ontario.

The Commissioners heard many recommendations concerning the changes that are needed in Ontario secondary schools if, indeed, they are to prepare students satisfactorily for their immediate post-secondary pursuits and, ultimately, to take their place in society. Among the many criticisms, we heard that secondary schools were inflexible and students felt that many programs were irrelevant to their future needs. They wanted improved guidance and counselling and, in general, higher expectations, more rigorous and interesting programs. It was felt that secondary schools did a better job of preparing university-bound students than the majority of students who did not go on to university. As Commissioners, we had a lot to say about secondary education and did recognize the need for a more large-scale review of the system.

We will not, in this paper, outline the many proposals of this reform initiative. We will, however, comment on a few issues:

1. We agree wholeheartedly with the renewed focus on guidance and career education, cooperative education, and work experience.

2. If indeed the recommendations regarding teacher-advisor system are implemented, we do see great benefits accruing to students. The establishment of an Annual Education Plan

and the counselling and parental involvement related to this, if done in a systematic way, can assist students in the career decision-making process.

3. We worry that if students are expected to decide on a destination too soon in their careers, this could end up being another form of streaming that could be detrimental to our students. At best, thirteen- to fifteen-year-old students are still in the tentative phase of career decision making — a period in which they change their minds very often as they learn more about their interests, abilities, values, and dispositions.

4. We were frankly disappointed with the section of the report entitled "Antidiscrimination Education." It is obvious that the Ministry is moving away from the policies that are currently in place. The view being advanced is that students need equal opportunity and equal access — nothing is mentioned about student achievement in terms of equity of outcome. The section fails to name and address issues of racism or sexism, nor does it mention the need to identify and address the many barriers to success for visible minority and students who live in poverty.

The Ministry of Education and Training cannot ignore the impact of all forms of discrimination on some students, which put them in double or even triple jeopardy.

The Ministry must insist that boards pay special attention to the issue of underachievement of visible minority and poor children. Our education system will never achieve greatness if certain groups continue to experience failure.

D. Conclusion

The issues identified earlier in this paper — those that deal specifically with the education of students of African Heritage — have been identified in study after study and most recently in an extensive analytical work by George Dei (1995). The issues have been studied ad infinitum and recommendations have been made ad nauseam. It is true that schools cannot improve education all by themselves. The African proverb that was mentioned earlier, "It take the whole village to raise a child," has gained increasing currency in Canadian education. Parents and communities have a role, as do politicians, but as educators our primary role is teaching and our primary goal is academic achievement for all students.

The Report of the Royal Commission on Learning was aptly titled, For the Love of Learning. The Commissioners observed:

> We must nurture curiosity, make learning interesting and challenging, and help youngsters, especially in their early years, to appreciate the challenges and pleasures of learning. Only then can we develop citizens with a sense of obligation to do their personal best, not merely for a mark or a paycheque, but because they derive satisfaction from the challenge of working a problem through. (Volume 1, page 68)

The Commissioners elaborated further:

> If the school offers little support in a student's home language or cultural heritage, if students do not see themselves reflected in the curriculum or among the teaching staff, they may be less motivated to learn, less confident in themselves as learners, and therefore, less successful. (Volume 1, pages 69-70)

Much has been done, but much more remains to be done. The educational system must redouble its efforts to respond to the challenge of educating all students successfully. The Commission's report, and so many other reports, are in our hands. It is time to act decisively to ensure vigorous implementation of the recommendations of the Royal Commission on Learning in order to promote excellence and academic success for all students.

APPENDIX 1

SELECTED GOVERNMENT-COMMISSIONED REPORTS THAT PRE-DATE THE REPORT OF THE ROYAL COMMISSION ON LEARNING

1. The Hall/Dennis Report (1968)

The mandate of this report was to develop aims and objectives for education in Ontario and to recommend means by which these aims could be achieved.

2. The Secondary Education Review Project (SERP) (1981)

The mandate of this project was to examine secondary schools and develop a blueprint to lead secondary schools into the 21st century.

3. The Re-organization of Secondary Education (ROSE) (1982)

This was the response of the Ministry of Education to the SERP Report.

4. The McDonald Commission (1985)

This report dealt with the financing of elementary and secondary education.

5. The Report of the Commission of Private Schools in Ontario (1985)

The mandate of this Commission was to identify and comment on possible alternative forms of governance, public funding, existing and possible relationships between private elementary and secondary schools and school boards and to make recommendations for changes in the governance of private schools in Ontario.

6. The Radwanski Report (1987)

The mandate was to make education relevant to the needs of young people and to the realities of the labour market, and to recommend ways by which the drop-out rate could be reduced.

7. The Select Committee Reports (1989-90)

The Select Committee reports dealt with the goals of education, modifications to the school day and school year, education finance and early childhood education.

8. The Premier' Council Reports (1988-89)

As reflected in their titles, these reports were: *Competing in the New Global Economy and People* and Skills: *A Review of Education, Training and Labour Adjustment Issues in Ontario.*

9. The Report of the French Language Governance Advisory Group (The Cousineau Report) (1991)

The mandate of this committee was to recommend ways and means to implement French Language governance in Ontario

10. The Stephen Lewis Report (1992)

The mandate was to advise the government on race relations.

REFERENCES

Dei, George J. Sefa with Holmes, L., McIssac E. & Campbell, R. (1995), *Drop Out or Push Out: The Dynamics of Black Students' Disengagement from School*. Toronto, The Ontario Institute for Studies in Education.

Drucker, Peter F. (1993) *Post-Capitalist Society*. New York, Harper Business.

Four-Level Government/African Canadian Community Working Group (1992). *Towards a New Beginning: Report on Metropolitan Black Canadian Community Concerns*. Toronto. Toronto Neighbourhoods Committee.

Glaze, Avis (1994) "Eight Educational Leadership Imperatives." in *InnoVations in Black Education in Canada*. Vincent D'Oyley, (editor) National Council of Black Educators of Canada, Toronto, Umbrella Press.

— (1993) "Life Roles, Life Chances and Career Education: The Equity Imperative". In Education *and Work*. David Corson and Stephen B. Lawton (editors). Toronto, The Ontario Institute for Studies in Education.

Government of Ontario (1968) Living *and Learning: The Provincial Committee on the Aims and Objectives for Education*. Toronto.

Lewis, Stephen (1992) "Dear Bob." Letter to the Premier. Toronto.

Ontario Ministry of Education (1980) Race, *Religion and Culture in Ontario School Materials: Suggestions for Authors and Publishers*, Toronto, Ontario Ministry of Education.

Radwanski, George (1987) *Ontario Study of the Relevance of Education and the Issue of Drop-outs.* Ontario Ministry of Education.

Royal Commission on Learning. (1994) For *the Love of Learning.* Toronto, Oueen's Printer for Ontario.

Avis Glaze on Principals

THE PRINCIPAL AS EFFECTIVE
COMMUNICATOR
CPCO

By Dr. Avis Glaze

As educational leaders, you as principals are strategically positioned to shape the direction of education and of society as a whole. You have aspired to and have been chosen to assume the daunting task of educating the nation's children. You are a powerful influence in the lives of students, equipping them with the knowledge, skills, attitudes, dispositions, sensibilities, and character attributes necessary for responsible and engaged citizenship. You are responsible for creating safe havens, caring and demanding learning cultures, and effective schools that emphasize both excellence and equity. You create the conditions for success in teaching, learning, and student achievement and you engage parents and communities in meaningful ways to support learning. With all that you make happen in your schools, you also serve as leaders in your communities.

To accomplish all of these expectations, principals must possess outstanding communication skills. In fact, I would argue that strong communication skills, both verbal and nonverbal, are important components of effective leadership. The following are a few of these essential people skills that should be taught in a systematic and intentional manner in leadership development programs. The most effective principals possess these interpersonal competencies and are known for their ability to integrate them into their daily interactions with people. These skills are often described as "soft skills." But in leadership, soft skills are often the hardest skills to learn and demonstrate. Many careers have been shattered because of the absence of these skills and the inability to work effectively with people and to motivate them toward the achievement of strategic goals and organizational directions.

These soft skills include, but are not limited to, the ability to demonstrate:

- Positive regard

- Active listening

- Empathic understanding

- Meaningful questioning

- Respectful assertiveness

- Constructive confrontation

- Effective feedback, and

- Willingness to accept criticism

While all of the above aspects of effective communication are important, I encourage principals not underestimate the importance of non-verbal communication generally. All leaders should take concrete steps to obtain feedback from a trusted colleague on their non-verbal styles and to understand how these styles affect the people they lead. The old saying "your actions speak so loudly I can hardly hear what you are saying" is a message that principals who strive to achieve mastery in this important aspect of leadership should bear in mind.

But it is also true that the further we climb up the ladder of success, the less likely we are to get meaningful critiques, or what is often described as negative feedback, from those we supervise directly or those on the lower rungs of the organizational hierarchy. As a young administrator, my strategy was to select a few people whose opinions I trusted and valued and to ask them to give me feedback on all aspects of my behaviour. I also learned to give feedback and accept it non-defensively from my counsellor education training. This required the ability to listen without interrupting or without the "Yes...but..." or "Yabuts" that often demonstrate an unwillingness to accept criticism. In fact, the ability to accept criticism without defensiveness is one of the most important interpersonal skills. The good news is that these skills can be taught effectively.

I remember well a teacher candidate in a course I developed in a faculty of education on human relations in education telling me that my "resting face" made me appear to be angry. I was frankly not aware of this. I went home that evening and tried to observe my "resting face" in the mirror. I was not happy at all with what I saw. She was correct! I have never forgotten that feedback and how it contributed to my personal growth and self-awareness.

In this brief article, the focus of my comments will be on communication with parents with the caveat that good communication also equals good public relations. The two are inextricably linked.

One of my colleagues, Dr. Jim Watt, had a background in both marketing and education. He used to stress the point that the public has a right to know as a fundamental premise of good public relations. For him, public relations is not the same as parent relations, nor is it about dispensing information or simply dealing in positives. He emphasized that it is not merely publicity, nor propaganda, nor the generation of a cosmetic effect. Instead, public relations involve three things — the ability to create and foster:

- Dialogue
- Access, and
- Involvement

The notion that dialogue is an essential component of communication is important for school leaders. It suggests that communication is more than the usual two-way communication; in school systems, it is multi-pronged and multi-faceted. It has many layers. It is not simply about issuing edicts and directives. The notion of access suggests that effective principals make themselves accessible to the people they serve. It does not take long to determine whether or not a principal is accessible when one visits a school. It was known, for example, that Dr. Jim Watt, who I mentioned earlier, would be in his school every Wednesday evening until at least 9 p.m. for the sole purpose of making himself more accessible to the public. With that knowledge, community members would drop in to see him if they had a question or concern. In addition to regular appointments, which individuals could make at any time, he certainly practised what he preached about dialogue, access, and involvement.

We also know that successful principals work assiduously at fostering outreach and engagement with their diverse communities and encourage involvement in the life of the school. Within our diverse contexts, principals can lead with confidence when they develop good relations with these communities and are able to call on members to assist them with resolving issues that confront them. Human rights are very important in Canadian society. Today's principals communicate in many languages with their communities. They have access to the opinion leaders to whom they can refer questions about the tenets of a particular religion, for example. As a superintendent, I dealt with a situation in which a student had announced emphatically that a requirement was "against my religion." That principal was hesitant to confront that situation because of the implication of not being sensitive to religious beliefs. But the principals who engage and communicate regularly with their diverse populations certainly develop confidence in dealing with sensitive issues. This happens, not because they have all the information at hand, but because they have established clear lines of communication and have made in-roads into the communities. They can call on community leaders to assist with the school's understanding of the issues under discussion.

An effective principal communicates with parents in many ways, the most effective of which is face to face communication. This is essential not only when conflicts arise but on a regular basis. Parents expect timely communication, especially about the progress of children. Most importantly, they want to know about the first signs of attendance problems or lack of improvement in achievement. They need to know how their children are doing generally, including behavioural challenges and whether or not students are handing in assignments on time.

When I was a secondary vice principal, I worked with a teacher who was near retirement. Throughout his years in education, every night he took home the phone numbers of three students with the intention of calling their parents and giving them a progress report. Parents appreciated this very much. Quite often, it was good news: "Pradesh is improving in math" or "Charlene is doing very well this term" or "It is a pleasure to have Edwardo in my class." This teacher was a consummate communicator who became legendary in his ability to keep parents informed about their children's progress in school.

One of the issues I had to deal with as a secondary school vice-principal was the failure of a student at the end of a school year in a non-semestered program. The parents said that they had no idea that the student was at risk of not completing the credit successfully. Mind you, this was many years ago. The principals I know today take communication, especially about academic progress, quite seriously. But the point I would like to make is that parents and students should know, in a timely manner, about what they are learning, how they are doing and what it takes to get them to the next level. I have been most impressed with schools in which students are able to articulate their learning goals, how they are doing, and what they need to do next. In these situations, their teachers have invariably provided them with precise and timely feedback — an essential component of the work of researchers such as John Hattie (2012) on visible learning. His findings of what works in improving student achievement and their relative effect sizes should become a part of every principal's repertoire.

In an effort to communicate effectively, one size certainly does not fit all circumstances. It is important for principals to reflect on the key reasons for communicating and the most effective ways to communicate their messages. Is it designed to inform, to disseminate information, to solicit input or feedback, to make requests, or to rally a group towards a desired goal? Is it a call to action or is it simply to keep parents and guardians informed about a student's progress? Is it to inform the community about the state of their education system or is to provide a report card to the public on the achievement of stated goals and priorities? Is it to share information that will help to build public confidence in the education system and in the services being provided?

Some school districts have communications officers. My experience is that these individuals, many of whom have specialized training, are an excellent resource. They can help prevent or minimize the impact of what can result when we do not have training in public and media relations or when we are not aware of the pitfalls that may arise from insufficient or inadequate communication.

My advice to school districts is to offer training in public and media relations for current and future leaders. Some districts are already doing this. Aspiring or new principals are encouraged to make a habit of soliciting input from individuals who have a background in communications and public relations. It is wise to seek out their advice in the early stages of planning and to confer with them regularly as a situation, project, or initiative evolves. If you do not have this resource at your disposal, I would recommend that you confer with individuals in neighbouring districts or businesses. They can, indeed, help prevent the need for the damage control that often results when communication goes awry.

The good news is that there are experienced colleagues and supervisors in all school districts who can provide the coaching and support necessary to resolve communication conflicts successfully. Handling these situations requires an openness to learn with and from your colleagues who have dealt with similar situations and have spent time reflecting on their problem resolution processes in light of the communications protocols that exist within some school districts. As well, principals who have developed support networks and who believe in teamwork and collaboration will always find solutions to address the challenges that inevitably arise.

References:

Gazda, George M. Asbury, Frank S. Balzer, Fred J. Childers, Phelps, Rosemary E. William C. Walters, Richard P. (1999) Human *Relations Development: A Manual for Educators*. Allyn and Bacon, MA.

Glaze, Avis; Mattingley, Ruth; Andrews, Rod. (2012) High *School Graduation: K-12 Strategies that Work*. Corwin, California.

Hattie, John (2012.) *Visible Learning for Teachers: Maximizing Impact on Learning*, Routledge, New York.

Avis Glaze:
Reflections on Receiving
the Robert Owen Award

REFLECTIONS ON RECEIVING
THE ROBERT OWEN AWARD

How appropriate it is for Mr. Michael Russell, Cabinet Secretary for Education, to enshrine in the history of Scottish education, the memory and legacy of Robert Owen. The Robert Owen Centre for Educational Change is, as Mr. Russell stated, a centre that will be "devoted to our understanding of how to improve the life chances of our young people." The vision is that this centre will be a window into the world, one in which others will learn with and from Scotland and further the cause of educational equity — a hallmark of Owen's legacy. This centre will promote successful practices and be a lighthouse for educators across the globe. It will further advance the cause of equity of outcomes and solidify Scotland's place in the global community.

What an honour it was for me to learn from Mr. Michael Russell, Cabinet Secretary, that I would receive the Robert Owen Award for education. I am grateful for this recognition and for the bold action in making me the first recipient.

As I read about Owen's beliefs, philosophies, and actions, I could not help but think of how fortunate I was to be associated with this great reformer. I see many parallels between what Robert Owen believed and out motivations as educators today. For example:

1. Robert Owen believed in the importance of education

It is also important for us to recognize the interconnectedness of a good education system and the development of the kind of society we want. A literate society with an educated citizenry is the life-blood of democracy. Society is dependent on the human capital that is nurtured by a good education system.

Robert Putnam (1993) once concluded that communities that succeeded socially and economically did not become civil because they were rich, but rather became rich because they were civil. The best predictors of success, he concluded, were strong traditions of civic engagement. Putnam described these aspects of civic engagement as social capital.

Teachers contribute to the development of a civil society. We enrich public participation and contribute to democracy building. We encourage responsible citizenship, giving students the skills to anticipate problems and to contribute to solutions. We also help them to understand what it means to be human in our increasingly interdependent world.

As educators, we must ensure that our country continues to be the embodiment of a civil society with strong social capital. Each day, within our classrooms, we create and contribute to the society that our children and grandchildren will inherit.

Literacy, one of the most important outcomes of schooling, is an investment in human capital. It is the foundation for future learning and success in school. It helps to secure a better livelihood and affects later educational and career choices. It makes possible future participation in society, and contributes to one's life chances, sense of personal fulfilment, and employability. Being literate is liberating and empowering. By focusing on educating young children, Robert Owen not only engaged in community development but he also made one of the best investments in the development of human capital and in the development of a civil society.

Owen's focus on literacy enhanced students' life chances. Because literacy is the gateway to all learning and an important means of social mobility, he made it possible for individuals to extricate themselves from a life of poverty. It follows, then, that, as teachers, we must recognize the potential of our publicly funded education system to bring about significant changes within our society.

I know that educators do not like to be compared to other professions because teaching is such a unique occupation. But I cannot resist the temptation of sharing the following perspective with the hope that it will stimulate vigorous debates in faculty lounges. Whittle (2005) said:

> In schools of the future leaders will assume highly consistent academic results the same way flight crews assume flawless performance, the same way doctors and patients now expect near perfection in certain basic procedures.
>
> In hospitals and airplanes, lives are on the line. In schools, the quality of those lives is determined. The standard should be the same.

3. Teachers today must educate hearts as well as minds. In this regard, character education offers great promise to achieve this goal

Character development is the deliberate effort to nurture the universal attributes upon which schools and communities find consensus. These attributes provide a standard for behaviour against which we hold ourselves accountable. They bind us together across socioeconomic, racial, religious, cultural, gender, and other lines that often divide people and communities. They form the basis for our relationships. Through character, we find common ground.

Character development continues to be an important aspect of schooling. Parents and business want schools to focus on character development to develop the habits of mind and heart that are necessary for the development of the important "soft skills" necessary for personal fulfilment and the success of interpersonal relationships.

Teachers have always been character developers. This is not a new initiative. What is new is that there should be a national focus on ensuring communities play a key role in determining the attributes upon which these programs are based and the recognition that when there is a whole school effort to focus on character attributes in all policies, programs, practices, and interactions, there is a positive impact on school culture. Achievement also increases as teachers spend more time on teaching and less on discipline.

In the early stages of implementation of character development programs in Ontario, we asked schools to send us anecdotal accounts of the effect that this initiative was having. A vice-principal sent us the following true story, which to my mind, represents character development in action:

> With the change-over to an electronic system for teacher absences, one morning, a grade six class ended up without a supply teacher. This information was unavailable to us in the office; we were unaware we had a grade 6 class without a teacher. After the opening exercises, and fifteen minutes into period one, a grade six student came to the office to report that their teacher had not come. I went to investigate with a great deal of trepidation. How many students would still be there? What would I do if some of them had slipped out of the school? What would I tell their parents?
>
> The class was at the far end of the school. All was quiet in the hall. When I entered the classroom, could you believe it? The students were busy writing and barely looked up to acknowledge that I had entered the room. What I

discovered was that a student had read the teacher's Daily Plan, wrote the instructions on the board for the class to follow and all were doing the work. They were working in groups, so that students who needed support were with others who could help them. When I congratulated them on their responsibility, with much relief, the answer was, "Miss, what did you expect? We're a character class!"

When character education is done well, it has the potential to further the goals related to student engagement, motivation, achievement, volunteerism, and citizenship.

Robert Owen had a very positive view of human nature. He acted consistently on his values and beliefs. He believed in the power of education to change society. What I admired most was the fact that he was not just interested in making money but in creating a new type of community at New Lanark. On many occasions, I have talked about the fact that schools should no longer aim to simply reflect community as we were taught years ago. Instead, we must be proactive in creating community. In fact, Drucker (1999) said:

> Society in all developed countries has become pluralist and is becoming more pluralist day by day....But all early pluralist societies destroyed themselves because no one took care of the common good. If our modern pluralist society is to escape the same fate, the leaders of all institutions will have to learn to be leaders beyond the walls. They will have to learn that it is not enough for them to lead their own institutions, though that is the first requirement. They will also have to learn to become leaders in the community. In fact, they will have to learn to create community.

As professionals, we will keep our optimism alive. We must continue to envisage a future that is bright and full of possibilities because we chose teaching as a profession. We are assiduous in our efforts to improve public confidence in our education systems. We stand on the shoulders of education reformers like Robert Owen and view the world through his lens of equity and social justice. If we choose to act on our beliefs, we will certainly uphold his legacy.

References

Peter Drucker, (1999) *Leading Beyond the Walls*

Levin, H.M. (1972). *The costs to the nation of inadequate education: A report prepared for the Select Committee on Equal Educational Opportunity of the United States Senate.* Washington, D.C.

Putnam, R.D. (1993). *The prosperous community: Social capital and public life. The American Prospect,* 13, 35–42.

Trudeau, P. E. (1994). *Memoirs.* Toronto: ON: McClelland & Stewart.

Whittle, C. (2005). *Crash course: Imagining a better future for public education.* New York: Penguin.

In Conversation with
Dr. Avis Glaze

IN CONVERSATION WITH
DR. AVIS GLAZE

Roderick Benns interviewed Avis Glaze on a range of issues, from literacy to extreme politics and hate, to poverty, policy, and some of the Canadian prime ministers she most admires. They also discussed her own legacy in education.

Benns: *What are the unique advantages you see in the Canadian education system?*

Glaze: Canada in general, and Ontario specifically, the province in which I worked for almost forty years, did not achieve its excellent reputation by chance. It came about as a result of targeted interventions and intentionality of purpose. Success can be attributed to a well thought out, research-informed strategy. As well, what is most impressive is that Ontario instituted a strategy that calls upon the ultimate in the professionalism of its teachers. When other countries were employing more negative and punitive approaches at that specific point in time, Ontario adopted a collaborative approach that focused on capacity building as the major strategy for improvement.

Other provinces are doing very well. British Columbia, where I now live, does well on international assessments. I have worked with educators in Nova Scotia and Prince Edward Island and have presented at conferences in other provinces. There are certainly pockets of excellence in all provinces. Our commitment must be to make every school a good school and every province an excellent province in which to educate our children.

It also means that we harnessed the energy of all key partners in developing and implementing this strategy. In retrospect, and knowing what happens in many countries across the globe, I must admit that we made the right decision and put together the right strategy. Instead of beating up on our teachers, calling them names as some governments did, we co-opted them, respected them, and built upon their professionalism by supporting them throughout the process.

As I work with some 40 countries and U.S. states, I am able to compare these strategies with what we are doing at home. We rejected the "shame and blame" or "one size fits all" approaches to education reform. We ensured that excellence and equity are not polar opposites — they go hand in hand. We continue to hold high expectations for all children, regardless of background or personal circumstances. We developed a common understanding, with concomitant actions to underscore the belief that poverty should not determine destiny. We focused on capacity building as the cornerstone for system improvement. We make leadership development a priority to ensure that all aspiring, beginning, and experienced leaders have the knowledge, skills, attitudes and dispositions necessary for leadership success.

We must have ways and means of monitoring ourselves. One of the strategies we used in Ontario was the School Effectiveness Framework. We developed this document as a means of self-evaluation. We could measure our behaviours and attitudes against the indicators of success that we identified. That self-analysis led to the identification of our strengths and the areas that needed improvement. Based on those findings, we then charted a course for continuous improvement.

There is no silver bullet. It is a multifaceted approach, but these are some of the unique strengths in the Canadian system.

Benns: *What are some of your disappointments, so far, in the way education in Canada or the Western World at large has been progressing?*

Glaze: I have been quite pleased with the improvement agenda of most countries. There is some consensus on the "what" but where there is disparity is on the "how." And to my mind, that is what really makes the difference.

There are still a few countries that do not use capacity building as the major lever or tool for improvement. Needless to say, those countries are simply spinning their wheels. They still believe in massive testing and outmoded notions of accountability. They believe that constantly weighing the pig will make it fat. They do not look at issues such as future trends, what students are like today, the needs of teachers, the importance of having educators participate fully in all improvement efforts and other such aspects of reform, in order to bring about change.

I am sometimes disappointed that many do not take the research findings about the importance of parental involvement seriously enough. In some jurisdictions, parental outreach and engagement is not receiving the attention that is required. Nor is student engagement. How can we improve education without the input of students?

Another issue that is very important to me is the topic of equity and inclusive education. Many provinces in Canada have well-developed strategies. They recognize the importance of diversity and have established strategies to ensure that all students succeed in school. Three of the protocols that I know well are the Ontario, Prince Edward Island, and Nova Scotia strategies. These are outstanding documents — fully supported by ministers of education at the time of their development. They are being implemented because the ministers are fully supportive and stand behind these expectations.

But not all provinces have collected data so that they have a clear picture of who the students are who are not succeeding.

If you don't know who the students are, you will not be able to take ameliorative steps. Some people are still thinking that you cannot "single out" any particular group. I would encourage them to begin to identify these groups and address their special needs with a sense of urgency. My common refrain — and the title of this book — is that the children cannot wait.

The issues I have been most concerned about are essentially human rights issues. If you look at any Human Rights Code in Canada, you will see the prohibited grounds — in other words, we cannot discriminate based on race, gender, place of origin, etc. I think we must also highlight socioeconomic status as an important area of concern because of the importance of the issue of poverty.

I care about the education of boys, just as as I grew concerned about girls in the 1980s. In fact, I did one of my research topics on the "Factors which influence the career aspirations and expectations of Ontario high school girls: implications for career education." I had that focus because I do believe that we do not do enough in a systematic way to ensure that students get the career preparation that they need in order to make these decisions that will affect their life chances in very profound ways. Still, too many women live in poverty. That still needs to change. But I do believe that we have not given boys and men the attention we gave to girls and women over the last 20 years. Mind you, some of my friends think that men are doing just fine in society. They still have most of the major high-status occupations and earn more than women. The wage disparity is still a very important issue. But we just need to look at some of our young men in society today. They appear to be rudderless. They, too, need support.

Other countries have identified this issue. I understand that Britain, for example, has targeted programs for working class white boys. What this says to us is that affirmative action is alive and well. We must give special attention and develop unique strategies for any group that is underperforming in our schools, or that is not doing well in society.

I am very conscious of the fact that I am aging. I am concerned about issues related to "seniors." I am now one of them. But I am still quite fortunate, having been a member of the Ontario Teachers' Pension Plan. I worry about the many individuals today who do not have pensions. With the high cost of living, I wonder what old age will be for them. Do they have a plan for long-term care? Will we ensure a basic income guarantee for all? Will we have the nurses and the doctors in all areas to address their needs? What about our children from indigenous groups? Are they being educated in a way that honours their values, customs, and traditions that will ensure success in school? Are we teaching qualities such as respect and empathy in our schools? Will our children be aware of the scientific inventions on the horizon and have the character attributes and values to address them in responsible ways? There are so many ethical questions today, from human and therapeutic cloning, food irradiation, stem cell research, nanotechnology, artificial human organs — and the list goes on.

When I am an old woman in a retirement or long term care home, will the students of today treat me with respect, affording me the dignity that I am sure I will crave at that age, and treat me as they would themselves want to be treated? Are we helping them to internalize the Golden Rule? Are we making sure that the education they are receiving is holistic in nature — focusing on issues such as character education, resilience, people skills, and values education?

I tend to be extremely impatient. Change for some groups is not happening fast enough. As educators, we must find a way to improve our schools from within. Change should not have to be imposed externally. We know what needs to be done. But this must be done with a sense of urgency, efficiently and effectively. Parents are expecting it. Politicians are demanding it. Our society requires it. We certainly have the will and the skills to make this happen. We cannot just accept the idea that it takes generations to bring about change. Ours is the generation that must make it happen faster.

Benns: *So much has changed when it comes to the written word, the way we communicate with one another, and how we access information. Do we need an expanded definition of what literacy is today?*

Glaze: Yes, it's very important that we move away from only understanding literacy as reading books and writing essays. There are so many different existing and emergent 'literacies" that we do need to broaden our ideas on this for if we are to educate young people successfully.

In the early days of the Literacy and Numeracy Secretariat, we worked as a team to gather definitions of literacy from across the globe. We crafted our own definition with the assistance of a few key people in the district, which included these words and phrases. The definition has grown over the years and has been refined significantly. These were some of our thoughts at the time:

> Literacy for the 21st century can be defined as the ability to use language and images in rich and varied forms to read, write, listen, view, represent, and think critically about ideas. It involves the capacity to access, manage, and evaluate information; to think imaginatively and analytically and to communicate thoughts and ideas effectively. Literacy includes critical thinking and reasoning to solve problems and make decisions related to issues of fairness, equity, and social justice, among others. It connects individuals and communities and is an essential tool for personal growth and active participation in a cohesive and democratic society. Literacy builds on prior knowledge, culture, and experiences in order to develop new knowledge and deeper understanding. It involves a lifelong continuum of learning for personal growth and active participation in our global society.

One of the authors who writes about this topic is Dustin Summey. If classrooms are to be considered effective in the 21st century, they must provide opportunities for students to experience, practice and apply these "literacies" in their daily work.

Summey has identified the following emergent literacies:

Computer Literacy: The ability to learn and use computers and related technology

Cultural Literacy: A certain level of exposure and familiarity with diverse cultures

Game Literacy: Diverse gaming experience and the ability to interpret games in many contexts

Media Literacy: Interpreting all meaning contained within media messages

Multiliteracies: Communication fluency across cultures, societies, and technological modalities

Multimedia Literacy: Using multimedia tools to convey information effectively

Network Literacy: Navigating, interacting, and discerning within virtual and human networks

Social Literacy: Thriving in diverse social contexts, both online and offline

Visual Literacy: Drawing meaning from visual depictions; also, to create such imagery

Web Literacy: Handling content and collaboration safely and productively online

Information Literacy: Locating, interpreting, organizing, and sharing information appropriately

New Literacies Online reading comprehension and learning skills, social adaptability

Digital Literacies Working intelligently with digital tools and data

Summey provides further examples of and applications for all of these literacies. Digital literacy, for example, is identified as one of the essential skills for managing information and communication in a digital world, incorporating skills such as:

- Locating and Filtering
- Sharing and Collaborating
- Organizing and Curating
- Creating and Generating
- Reusing and Repurposing

I have always said that literacy cuts across all subject areas, which means that all teachers are literacy teachers, in one form or another. Literacy is the gateway to all future learning. It is a major source of liberation for individuals. Life chances are truncated and democracy is compromised if we do not have literate young people who will play their part in creating a literate citizenry.

Benns: *Given how much has changed in the world, do we also need a more complete understanding of entrepreneurism?*

Glaze: Absolutely. I often quote Yong Zhao in this regard, who has written extensively on this topic. Zhao says that "high school students who exhibit creative personalities are more likely to drop out of high school than other students."

I fear — as I know Zhao does — that this is because we don't do enough to spark the creative and entrepreneurial spirit of youth. Entrepreneurs open doors not only for themselves but for others as well. They are problem solvers and risk takers. I think we need to do more than we are doing now to nurture creativity and the entrepreneurial spirit in our society.

Benns: *Despite our progress in the world, inevitably we see and hear incidences of extreme politics and hate. How do we address issues like hate in the future? What is the role of the educator in this regard?*

Glaze: I have always believed that respect and empathy should accompany any rigorous education program. This is part and parcel of strong character development, and so it must, therefore, be a mandatory part of education. This is the best way to counter the scourge of hate. It's hard to develop hatred with a mind that has been opened. For then children will have been taught at an early age to respect and value the dignity and worth of every human being in our society.

I like what author Elie Wiesel says on this. He says "the opposite of love is not hate, it's indifference." We cannot afford to be indifferent in a global society. This connects to issues such as people skills. It doesn't matter what field someone works in — at some point, each of us encounters other human beings, and it is imperative to know how to relate. These are things that should be taught. Our society is becoming increasingly diverse. Schools are laboratories of what effective human relations should look like, and this works against the premise of hate.

I also believe that resilience should be taught. Schools must also address issues such as philanthropy, altruism, volunteerism, community engagement, and community development. Schools must stay in close contact with parents, and both parents and educators should be aware of the warning signs of depression, another problem that more and more young people are facing today.

Another effective way would be to have teachers actively involved with race relations. Think about the environment and ecology. Teachers played a huge role in shifting environmental awareness. Even young students were coming home and telling their parents how to sort their blue boxes — teachers were a massive influence for the environmental movement, and there is no reason they couldn't also be this way for race relations. Let's empower teachers to act and encourage them to take this issue seriously, and we'll change the entire tone of these conversations.

Benns: *I want to ask you about the role of the educator when it comes to addressing the totality of student needs. This inevitably leads me to ask about poverty and the social structures we create. For instance, the kind of employment that is dominant now in Western nations is precarious in nature — part-time, without benefits, and there is a great rise in contract work. In the Greater Toronto Area, more than 50 percent of jobs are now classified this way. That means more parents are much poorer than they used to be and this affects how they can provide for their children. Do we need some kind of 'basic income guarantee' in our social safety net, during times of low or marginal employment, to combat this growing inequality in society?*

Glaze: Poverty creates so many disadvantages for students. It has been said that poverty is the enemy of education. So many are shortchanged if our society and our schools do not address these disadvantages in a systematic and intentional way. The educational literature makes clear the connections between poverty and educational outcomes.

One of my favourite writers, R. W. Connell, once said: "The best advice I would give to a poor child, eager to get ahead through education is to choose richer parents." Knowing Connell's work and lifetime commitment, I am sure that this was said tongue in cheek. It is clear that if students are from poor backgrounds, only the most determined, hardworking, and resilient will achieve success on their own and be able to extricate themselves from the social and economic conditions under which they were born.

We know that educators can make the difference for these young people. The caring teacher, with high expectations, who uses research-informed, high-impact strategies, can fully utilize the skills within his or her repertoire. These successful teachers know what works. They have both the skills and the will to make a difference in the lives of children.

I do think some form of basic income guarantee is warranted. Just how this is set up I will leave to the experts in social policy. But I must say, we do this for older people already, through the Guaranteed Income Supplement. We do it for children through the Canada Child Benefit. It's not a stretch, in my mind, to say let's ensure we take care of the basic needs of all Canadians with some kind of minimum income. Of course, we must balance this with the proper work incentives.

Benns: Is this being political? Should more educators get political?

Glaze: Let us not kid ourselves. Education is political. If we accept the view that politics is about how we allocate scarce resources, then we have no choice to be political. It means that we should, during these challenging times, stop saying "I am not political." In fact, I would encourage all teachers, leaders, parents, and community members to be political. It is about advocacy for the things we believe in. It means making our voices heard. It means standing up and making known the needs and aspirations of the children we chose to serve.

A few years ago, I reflected on the key characteristics of advocates. I concluded that educators are consummate advocates in their daily work in their communities. So much of what we have achieved is a result of some form of advocacy — people who take up causes that are important. And in most cases, these individuals do not benefit personally. They are fighting for causes outside of themselves — causes that will benefit others.

Many educators adopt a social advocacy position to improve conditions for the benefit of an individual or group. I've always liked Michael Fullan's assertion that "The starting point is not a system change, or change in those around us, but taking action ourselves. The challenge is to improve education in the only way it can be—through the day-to-day actions of empowered individuals."

Benns: *Within a global education and citizenship framework, let's talk about values for a moment. What are some non-negotiables for you when you think about citizenship?*

Glaze: When I applied for Canadian citizenship, I reflected at length on what citizenship means. I realized that it is a right, but more importantly, it is a privilege and a responsibility. I also saw it as an obligation that I could not take for granted.

We are all very fortunate to live in a country that respects the democratic process. In Canada, we are part of a governing process that serves our best interests. With citizenship come rights such as freedom of expression, religion, lifestyle, and many others. However, these rights come at a cost as we pledge to work collaboratively to maintain and improve the economic, political, and social aspects of our society. Our curriculum documents that address citizenship serve to address some of these points.

It is extremely important that, as a society, we act to engender the lofty ideals of a democratic citizen in our young people. Our public education system is making attempts to do just that. In many provinces across Canada, through mandatory courses in Civics and Canadian History, Law, or World Issues, our public education system is fostering positive and pro-social concepts of ideal citizenship among our younger generation. There is also a mandatory community service component for graduation in Ontario schools. Many other jurisdictions have adopted these measures.

It is important that, in a world dominated by popular culture in which very confusing messages reach our young people every day, we reinforce the need for an active and involved citizenry. We need to teach these important elements of democracy in a manner that engages young minds and harnesses their enthusiasm and optimism. Young people are full of passion and interest, and are willing to take on responsibilities that we, as adults, do not always provide for them. Let us realize their immense potential, and work with young people to sustain and create a world where citizenship and all its privileges, rights, and responsibilities are extended to all.

I also think of citizenship in my situation as an immigrant. When immigrants come to Canada, there is so much of our old country that we are allowed to keep within this context of diversity. We keep many of our customs, traditions, and ways of worshiping, among others. But I do believe that when it comes to prevailing values and the laws of Canada, there are non-negotiables for a nation. It means thinking seriously about what you were allowed to do in your old country and what your adopted country expects.

One case in point is the way women and girls are still treated in some societies. Some women are beaten when they do not fall in line. We have examples of girls being killed because they stray from family expectations regarding who they should date. Immigrants to Canada from countries where these behaviours are acceptable must understand that Canadian laws do not condone this treatment of women and girls. Admittedly, having worked in schools, I have seen numerous examples of inter-generational and inter-cultural conflicts, not only in immigrant communities, but also in the larger Canadian contexts. But I mention these in this context as there is a need for us to ensure that all immigrants are aware of the important cultural differences that can have a serious impact on their lives in Canada.

I also believe that immigrants to Canada must be encouraged to learn either English or French in addition to the many languages that they bring to make this country so rich and vibrant. Knowing the official languages would facilitate a sense of belonging and help immigrants avoid feeling isolated in Canadian society. Having a sense of belonging is so important for one's mental health, wellbeing, and ability to participate fully in the prosperity of this country.

This is all said from my perspective as a proud immigrant to Canada and one who will work assiduously to nurture these values and orientations in our young people so that we can all continue to create the country we have come to love and appreciate.

Benns: We've talked a lot about leadership in this book, and I know you believe that education is about nation building. So let me ask you about Canada's prime ministers. What prime ministers stand out for you and why?

Glaze: Canada has been blessed with good governance. It is one of the single greatest reasons our democracy is as successful as it is.

One of our greatest Canadian leaders, Sir Wilfrid Laurier, was also among the most eloquent. He said:

> "I say it is to our glory that the struggles of race are ended on Canadian soil. There is here now no other family than the human family, whatever the language they speak or the altars at which they kneel...Mighty nations, indeed, might well come to us to seek a lesson in justice and humanity.

What a wonderful way to illustrate a vision of Canada that I believe remains true to this day.

I also admire John Diefenbaker for his emphasis on human rights. He is particularly well known for standing up against the apartheid regime in South Africa in the early 1960s.

I also think of Pierre Trudeau. In his memoirs he was very eloquent when he wrote:

> "A country, after all, is not something you build as the pharaohs built the pyramids, and then leave standing there to defy eternity. A country is something that is built every day out of certain basic shared values."

Following in Diefenbaker's footsteps, I want to acknowledge Brian Mulroney's human rights leadership when it came to pressuring South Africa to dismantle apartheid. The U.S. and U.K. didn't want to use economic sanctions against South Africa, but Mulroney did. In rebuttal to U.K. Prime Minister Margaret Thatcher at a meeting, Mulroney said: "Margaret, in this great moral cause, I am going to place Canada clearly on the right side of history." And he did. When Nelson Mandela was released from prison, he chose Canada to make his first formal speech to a legislature because of the great leadership Mandela had experienced from Canada.

Another modern-day Prime Minister I admire very much is Paul Martin. He continues to do so much good work on behalf of indigenous Canadians. When he left office, he set up the Martin Aboriginal Education Initiative, which aims to improve elementary and secondary school education outcomes for indigenous Canadians. The organization is strongly research focused and is really making a difference.

Benns: *Who were some of the women you considered to be influential leaders in education in Ontario in the 1980s and 1990s, or even later?*

Glaze: There were many trailblazers in education in Ontario at this time, such as Pauline Laing, Joan Green, Pat Kincaid, Bev Freedman, and the late Sheila Roy. All were very supportive of other women in leadership, too. They paved the way for Women in Educational Administration in Ontario (WEAO), encouraging many females to assume their rightful place in the history of educational leadership. Many still see them as their role models, becoming leaders because of them. Pauline and Joan were directors of Durham District School Board and Toronto District School Board, respectively, an accomplishment not to be underestimated at the time.

Another individual who deserves special recognition is Dr. Lyn Sharratt, a consummate curriculum leader, and an exemplary teacher. We worked together in the York Region District School Board. I consider Lyn and her husband Jim our dear friends. Lyn's contributions to the area of curriculum and assessment have really made a difference to teachers and principals alike. She has become a prolific writer. One of her books, *Putting Faces on the Data*, is a must read for educators.

Cathy Abraham was a trustee at the time when I was at Kawartha Pine Ridge District School Board, and was already an effective leader even then. Now she is the current chair of the board. She is very bright and forward looking and has contributed significantly not only to the Kawartha board but at the provincial level, too.

Benns: *Do you continue to actively advocate for black students and if so in what ways?*

Glaze: Yes, absolutely. Even though I have moved from Ontario, I still continue my contributions to community development through participation in a new organization called Lifelong Leadership Institute (LLI). It's an organization committed to both inspiring and developing leadership with a focus on youth of African and Caribbean descent. In the early stages, I worked with Trevor Massey, co-chair of this committee. A lot of work has been done, and Trevor is now leading the interviews to select students who will participate in this program. In addition to the key role that Trevor plays, I also give full credit to other directors of the LLI who patiently stayed the course in making the organization a reality. Other directors include Pamela Appelt, Joe Halsted, Dr. Upton Allen, Dr. Carl James, Dr. Wendy Cukier, David Taylor, Linda Massey, Tka Pinnock, Nadine Spencer, Delford Blythe, and Kay Blair.

I am most grateful to Trevor, not only for his leadership of this project, but for his broader leadership within the African-Canadian community. I have not worked with a more organized, hardworking, and committed person. I also commend his wife, Linda Massey, who, in addition to her leadership at the Ontario Principals' Council, also finds time to play a pivotal role in helping our community to thrive.

Benns: *How did this LLI organization come about?*

Glaze: The genesis was the effort to celebrate Jamaica's golden anniversary in 2012 in the Greater Toronto Area. Among various ideas to plan the anniversary was a strong sentiment to include legacy initiatives that would have enduring benefits to the Jamaican-Canadian community — long after 2012. Leadership development met this test. The Future Leaders Institute initiative, now called the Lifelong Leadership Institute, was born. The primary goal of the LLI is to support the leadership and career aspirations of young Canadians of Jamaican and Caribbean heritage, up to age 30.

The signature program of the LLI will be Leadership by Design (LBD). This program envisions a patient course to leadership and career development as well as a strategic approach to closing the opportunity gap that so often hinders the growth and potential of so many of our youth. The program will select high school students from the Greater Toronto Area who are enrolled in Grade 10, and will offer developmental support spanning some seven or more years into university or college enrollment.

The directors of the LBD program are committed to continuous learning and improvement, and this will be facilitated by research support from a Ph.D. candidate from the Faculty of Education at York University.

Benns: *In terms of collective impact, your role as chief student achievement officer of Ontario and founding CEO of the Literacy and Numeracy Secretariat was a key position to be in. Considering that Ontario has the same population as all of Norway and*

Switzerland combined — more than 13 million people — it's clear this was a big mandate. How important was your selection of staff when it came to running this large organization?

Glaze: I knew this would be crucial when I first took over LNS. I had the good fortune of being able to hire all of my own staff. I thought carefully about the person who I would choose to work closest with me, as my associate. I looked around for some time, observed several people who already had a positive reputation in terms of their knowledge of curriculum, how they worked with people, and their commitment to continuous learning and improvement. Ego strength (not egomania), confidence, as well as a positive view of human nature were also important to me in a leader. I do believe strongly that these factors affect our supervisory behaviour and the way we lead others.

The person I invited to work as my associate was Ruth Mattingley. She was bright, supportive and non-competitive. She demonstrated moral leadership, and she was — and continues to be — an inveterate learner. That was one of my best decisions. Ruth exceeded my expectations in the role and should take great pride in contributing significantly to the success of the Secretariat.

I must say also, that I believe I hired the best staff one could ever have. I think of all the student achievement officers, the research and data staff, the community outreach staff and those who did the daily operations of the Secretariat with such fondness and admiration. They worked hard and achieved a great deal. They were the brightest and the best that Ontario had to offer.

I shouldn't stop at LNS in reflecting on this. I also think of many people who supported me and my work along the way: Dr. Pamela Appelt, Trevor and Linda Massey, Tessa Benn Ireland, Pat Howell, Dr. Jean Augustine, Dr. Mary Anne Chambers, Susan La Rosa, the late Erika Rimkus, Dr. Ernie Salmon, Dr. Maurice Edwards, Donnette Strickland Nurse and my colleagues from Church Teachers' College and the University of the West Indies in Jamaica; Dr. Inez Elliston and the members of my women's group — the Tiger Lillies, who met monthly at each other's homes for dinner. These women were high achievers and community-oriented. They still serve as outstanding role models for young women in general and young black women in particular. I'm sure I have missed others.

I belonged to many other organizations — Canadian Federation of University women, Black Educator's Group, Jamaican Canadian Federation, principals' associations, supervisory officers, women's groups, guidance counsellors, and other professional organizations. I worked with so many people whose generosity I will always remember. My administrative assistants in all the places I worked taught me so much. I would not have learned how to use computers, for example, without the patience of these women. I could never have been successful without them.

Let me not forget the custodians in all the places in which I have worked. Those in schools play such a pivotal role, not the least of which is as confidante and counsellor to many students. Whenever I make lasagna, I think of the custodian who gave me the recipe and, on more than one occasion, walked me through the steps of how to make a good lasagna. I loved the people with whom I worked. I still think of them and their families. I wonder how life is treating them. Are they happy? Have their children grown up to be productive citizens? Are they in good health? Have they prepared well for their retirement?

Throughout my career, I have put people first. In the workplace, I tried to treat them like family. I can only hope that they know how much I care about their well-being.

Benns: *Where do we go from here in education? What is the future role of an educator?*

Glaze: Education continues to be the lifeblood of our democracy. I continue to encourage my colleagues in education to persist in improving education from the inside out, to keep on pushing the boundaries for change and to take education systems to new heights of attainment. I am very optimistic about the future of education and the role that we will continue to play to address even the seemingly most intractable problems and challenges. For me, we now know more that we have ever known about what works and what it takes to improve with a sense of urgency. We now have a rich body of research and the knowledge that all children can learn and achieve with proper teaching and effective leadership.

I often think of the words of Larry Lazotte, one of the stalwarts in education. He said, "If you can find a good school without an effective principal, please call me collect." I would imagine that Larry does not receive many calls on this topic. I know that we do have many teacher leaders who are working wonders in our schools. But we still need strong leadership at all levels to bring about the improvements that we all want.

It is now time for us to take stock of our progress, savour this, and identify what remains to be done. We have achieved a lot in recent years and we must continue to build upon those successes. But we must also admit that not all students, from all backgrounds, are achieving at their potential. I mentioned earlier that I am concerned that our boys are not doing as well as they should in some jurisdictions. Many are falling behind. Children in special education programs must not spend their school careers in these programs. They are not meant to be a permanent placement. They should be revolving doors where students are admitted when they need help and are demitted regularly.

Character education needs to be a mandatory part of all activities, programs, and interactions. More students need to have access to career development programs where they learn the age-related tasks related to the career decision-making process. They need help with determining their interests, aptitudes, and dispositions, pulling these together to identify their areas of focus for the next stage of their education. More students need opportunities in their communities to learn the skills that employers want or that will help them to succeed in post-secondary education, and indeed in life. They need to explore the wide array of career options open to them, including the trades, colleges, and universities, from apprenticeship programs to entrepreneurial studies, and soft skills development.

Benns: *When you look back at your life and consider your own legacy, what do you want parents and educators to remember or say about Avis Glaze?*

Glaze: I want them to know how much I cared about the well-being and life chances of all the children I taught. I always put the needs of students first — sometimes even committing what others called "career limiting" actions on behalf of children. I fought for programs for expelled students so they could get their high school diploma. I advocated for pregnant girls to be able to continue their education. I conducted research on high school girls, proposing programs to enhance their aspirations and expectations and to receive the career education they needed without the constraints of conditioning or sex role ideology.

For adults, there were leadership development programs, special training in emotional intelligence, overseas immersion programs to learn about other school systems, community development initiatives to build character in schools, community, and workplaces. Champions for Youth programs to help children in trouble with the law. Programs for immigrant students, aspiring teachers, principal development, and programs for superintendents. Parent education programs and conferences for parents and community members were also designed to create stronger ties and build coalitions and alliances between the schools, parents, and communities.

It was also important to contribute to my own African-Canadian community. Many students, over a ten-year timeframe, received yearly scholarships to attend universities. I have had the pleasure of meeting many of these students and seeing how they benefited from these programs.

I have often told the story of hearing a young man play the violin at a public function. I was so impressed that I accosted him after the show and asked him to play at my wedding. He came to the wedding and serenaded the attendees.

It wasn't until much later that he said, "I don't think you remember me."

"Do remind me," I said.

"I received one of your scholarships to university!" was his response.

At that moment, it was driven home to me how important it is to support young people within our community through scholarships for post-secondary studies.

My grandmother was certainly not wrong when she urged us to "lift others as you climb."

Comments from around the world about Dr. Avis Glaze

ON AVIS

"Avis Glaze is an educational international treasure. She is ecumenical in thought, equitable in words and action, with character that is to be embraced. This biography is evidence of an enlightened individual whose wisdom has made a difference to education throughout the world. The book is a rare glimpse into the compelling life of a person whose leadership has had a profound influence on the lives of students and adults alike. Over close to 30 years I have witnessed her influence."

Bill Hogarth

"Avis Glaze is an inspirational and visionary leader. She was the architect for educational reform in schools across Ontario. Avis orchestrated the implementation of high impact strategies that resulted in not only improving student literacy and numeracy results in Ontario schools but also resulted in closing achievement gaps. She instilled a sense of urgency and inspired educators across the province to help all children succeed. Avis' life work has resulted in improving the life choices and chances for thousands of students."

Ruth Mattingley
Former Senior Executive Officer — Literacy and Numeracy Secretariat
Ontario Ministry of Education

"She inspires audiences with her passion and innovative leadership and her commitment to the well-being of every single child."

Bob Cook
Former Director of Education and Cultural Services
West Dunbartonshire Council, Scotland

"A recurring theme in the narratives of our presence in Canada as black people — as told (or written) for us, by us — is to re-assert our long and consistent contributions to the economic, social, cultural, political and educational development of Canada over the years. This is even more significant when we think of the significant roles that black educators like Dr. Avis Glaze have played in the schooling and education of Canadians. In particular, Dr. Glaze has been quite influential throughout the whole system of education — specifically, in her role as teacher in schools and universities, her leadership positions in school boards, her contribution to educational discourses through research and publications, and as a foundational leader in the Ministry of Education. A record of Dr. Glaze's life and work is worth having — for not only will it inspire, it will also provide valuable insights for what is useful to know if we are to continue making our contributions guided by her example.

Carl E. James, PhD, FRSC.
Professor & Director York Centre for Education & Community
York University, Toronto

The first time I saw Avis Glaze speak, I turned to my colleague immediately and said, "That woman is a powerhouse!" That initial impression has proved true many times over in Avis' impactful work in Ontario, Canada and around the world. Avis' leadership as Ontario's first Chief Student Achievement Officer and Founding CEO of the Literacy and Numeracy Secretariat played a pivotal role in improving student achievement in Ontario. Her world renowned reputation as a thought leader on system leadership, capacity building, character development and equity of outcomes for all students, takes her around the world working with governments to increase success for all learners. Curriculum Services Canada is honoured to have Dr. Avis Glaze as our first International Program Advisor.

Amy Coupal, Chief Executive Officer
Curriculum Services Canada

Like so many others, I have felt privileged to work with and learn from Avis. Each opportunity to do so leaves me with deeper knowledge, greater motivation and a stronger sense of purpose than before. This is Avis' true gift, to leave educators inspired by her commitment and passion, while empowering them to access and develop their own. Her style, the perfect balance of pressure and support, challenges us all to bring our best for the learners we serve every day, and then a little bit more.

-Debbie Davidson, Director of International Partnerships
Curriculum Services Canada

Avis is able to inspire and empower people. In her speeches and lectures she helps you understand things more clearly and work for the better future with enthusiasm and hope.

Irmeli Halinen
Head of Curriculum Development
Finnish National Board of Education
Hakaniemenranta 6
00531 Helsinki
Finland

Over these long years Dr. Avis Glaze has helped shape critical debates in Ontario and Canadian schooling and education. Her intellectual contributions to scholarship and research have extended beyond Canadian shores to reach international borders. She has been a pillar of great intellect, a scholar filled with critical ideas for promoting equity, social justice and inclusivity in schools. Many of us are deeply indebted to her scholarship, rich policy insights and her generosity to nurture emerging scholars in the field of contemporary education.

George J Sefa Dei
Professor of Social Justice Education & Director
Centre for Integrative Anti-Racism Studies
Ontario Institute for Studies in Education of the University of Toronto.
2015 Carnegie African Diaspora Fellow.

The account of your career is genuine and inspiring to young educators, especially those with less privileged backgrounds — they can see that they too have a moral purpose to ensure a good education for every child. One of the highlights of your career has been your ability to recognize, motivate and support other leaders to maximize their impact.

Dr. Joanne Robinson
Director of Professional Learning, Education Leadership Canada
CEO, International School Leadership
ONTARIO PRINCIPALS' COUNCIL

"Dr. Avis Glaze is a true professional in the field of education. Even the most difficult issues are easy to understand in her presentation."

Lauri Halla
Principal
Helsinki, Finland

"Dr. Avis Glaze is one of the most engaging, astute and energizing speakers we have invited to speak in the Caribbean. Her fascinating, insightful and effective presentations propel diverse audiences into action as individuals raise the bar for their future performance."

Sandra Welch Farrell
CEO, SWF and Company
Trinidad and Tobago

"Dr. Glaze has been a visionary in the field of character education. She is in demand for speaking engagements internationally because of her pioneering initiatives. She has been my inspiration."

Jacqueline Jones
Teacher and National Trainer
Eunice Kennedy Shriver Community of Caring
Baltimore, Maryland, USA

"Avis is highly regarded. She continues to provide outstanding opportunities for development and sharing across the province and globally. When she speaks, people listen, as they know that Avis always puts the needs of students first. Every presentation Avis makes is inspirational and motivating, giving every participant an even greater sense of urgency to improve his or her teaching on behalf of students. She provides every member in her audience an opportunity to truly see themselves reflected in what she is saying. More importantly, Avis has the unique gift of being able to validate the excellence in teaching while at the same time providing opportunities to reflect on practice that needs additional attention. She is truly a visionary in our time."

Larry Hope,
Director of Education
Trillium Lakelands District School Board

"Dr. Avis Glaze is a warm, caring person who truly values community outreach and parental engagement in education. Under her leadership, the Kawartha Pine Ridge District School Board (KPR) introduced several special initiatives. These included establishment of:

- an annual parent conference, to bring together parents and school council members to learn and share best practices

- a volunteer program encouraging community members and staff at the Education Centre to spend half a day of work time each month, volunteering in schools

- the Accolades program, which recognizes outstanding students, staff and volunteers with a special certificate presented at a Board meeting.

Avis also championed the introduction of intentional character development in our schools, involving the community in identifying the 10 positive character attributes on which our schools should focus."

Judy Malfara
Communications Officer-School Liaison
Kawartha Pine Ridge District School Board

"Her broad record of experience...combined with her impressive grace, eloquence, and intelligence produces a valuable and transformative speaker."

W. Berkowitz, Ph.D.

"She inspires audiences large and small with her passion for education and her commitment to the welfare of every child."

Bob Cook
Former Director of Education and Cultural Services
West Dunbartonshire Council, Scotland

"...there are few educators in the world who can match her leadership qualities and ability to teach others."

Michael Fullan

"Avis is an outstanding presenter, thinker, synthesizer, energizer and most significantly, leader of people."

Trevor Radloff
Director, School Effectiveness and Support
Adelaide, South Australia

Dr. Avis Glaze is the consummate educator. Her insatiable love of learning, uncompromised high standards and ability to communicate her beliefs passionately to others makes her writing a scholarly and current source of reflection. Always creative and thoughtful, the Avis Glaze Letters to Educators inspire and engage us to deliberately pause and reflect deeply on our moral imperative: to educate all of our children!"

Dr. Lyn Sharratt
Research Associate
York Region District School Board
North Toronto, Canada

Her passionate commitment to every student's improved achievement in a context of rapid organizational change has served to influence public policy as well as school and system leadership locally, nationally, and internationally for many years.

Dr. Denese Belchetz
Coordinating Superintendent of Education
York Region District School Board
Ontario, Canada

As an international educator, Avis listens to all of the stakeholders in education — particularly those who work directly with students. She has never forgotten her roots as a classroom teacher. The Avis Glaze Letters to Educators represent a culmination of Avis' experiences. They affirm what we are doing well in our classrooms, motivate us to work towards continued student success and inspire us to become leaders in our schools.

Teachers will find these letters supportive of their work and applicable to their classroom practice. As a teacher, I know that I will use these letters to enhance my teaching and to help us all take our schools to new levels of effectiveness."

Rachelle Mack
Teacher/Facilitator of Technology
Clarington Central Secondary School

"Avis Glaze has made outstanding contributions to education around the globe. Her powerful insights, drawn from a remarkable career, are presented with passion and genuine commitment. She inspires everyone fortunate to work with her and her influence will improve learning for future generations."

Alan Boyle
Leannta Education Associates
London, England

Avis is one of those rare individuals who can inspire an audience into believing that anything is possible — in the interests of young people. Her commitment, dedication and determination shine through all that she says and does; for Avis only the best would be good enough for Ontario's future citizens."

Marion J Matchett
Chief Inspector Northern Ireland

"Principals across Ontario have a deep respect for Avis. She has influenced the provincial direction of education for many years and has been a mentor to many future leaders. Her presentations are in great demand because of her ability to motivate and inspire all of us."

Joanne Robinson
Ontario Principals' Council
Education Leadership Canada

"As Leader of the Canadian Delegation at the UNESCO conference on Inclusive Education in Riga, Latvia, you made your country proud. Everyone commented on your presentation at the plenary session. It was truly exemplary!"

Dr. Mary M. Khimulu
Ambassador & Permanent Delegate of Kenya to UNESCO Paris, France

"When considering the work of LNS in total, one predominant theme emerged: in partnership with school boards, there has been a significant shift in the future of Ontario schools that is focused on enabling the success of all students. There has also been sustained improvement in student achievement.

These are major accomplishments... These efforts have had a positive impact in school boards and schools. LNS has created and sustained a "Sense of Urgency" that permeates the educational language being spoken throughout boards. This sense is not diminishing but rather is growing. At the same time, there is a general sense that the Ministry of Education, through the LNS, is providing much needed resources and opportunities that boards require to move their schools forward. Overall, the LNS is providing a valuable service, supporting the education of Ontario's children. This model is effective and the service should continue...Dr. Glaze has been a public face of the LNS, providing a consistent and persuasive message across the province. This has resulted in strong "brand recognition" for the LNS, with a consistent message from a well-recognized and respected educator..."

Excerpt, from the Evaluation of the Literacy and Numeracy Secretariat (2007) Canadian Language & Literacy Network (CLLRNet)

Dr. Avis Glaze is an extraordinary speaker. She speaks passionately and from the heart. Creating highly literate learning communities which value respect, responsibility, integrity and courage within a civil society is her key message. Her concern for the roles that educators play in preparing our youth to be the stewards of our Earth and the leaders of our future is clearly expressed in her talks."

Kelly Guichon, Chair, Delta School District British Columbia, Canada

"The work of the Literacy and Numeracy Secretariat over the last three years has had strong measurable impact across the province. Educators at all levels have become increasingly focussed on student achievement in reading, writing and mathematics, and all students and communities have benefited as a result. As well, the focus that you personally have *brought to Character Education has strengthened the ability of Boards to address significant issues for students and their communities. You can feel confident that this momentum will not be lost, and that the progress that you have driven will continue.*

·**Gerry Connelly**, Director of Education Toronto District School Board

AWARDS OF EXCELLENCE

Robert Owen Award: For character development, the first of its kind offered in Scotland.

Outstanding Contribution to Education Award 2008: In recognition of significant contribution to public education in Ontario.
Ontario Principals' Council, Toronto, Ontario

The Sandy McDonnell Lifetime Achievement Award for Character Education 2008: For initiating and transforming character education in Ontario.
Character Education Partnership (CEP)
Washington, D.C., U.S.A.

Outstanding Achievement Award 2008 In recognition of many years of dedication and service to the promotion of character development in school districts across Canada)
National Character Education Conference

The Arbor Award 2008: For outstanding service.
University of Toronto

Leadership in Education Award 2008: To recognize individuals whose innovation, leadership and exceptional contribution have made a difference in the education community of the province of Ontario.
Faculty of Education, University of Ottawa

Honourary Doctor of Laws 2008: For outstanding contribution to education in Ontario and Canada.
University of Windsor

Honourary Doctor of Laws 2008: For outstanding contribution to education, The University of Ontario Institute of Technology (UOIT).

Honouree — The Official Black History Legacy Poster 2007K One of three women featured by artist Robert Small, including Her Excellency the Right Honourable Michaëlle Jean, Governor General of Canada.
Toronto District School Board School
Trustee and Community Activist

York Regional Police 2007 Special recognition for service to community.

Toronto Police Services 2007: Special recognition for service to community.

Honourary Doctorate in Education — Nipissing University 2007: For outstanding contribution to education.

Amethyst Award 2007: While serving as CEO, the Literacy and Numeracy Secretariat was honoured with the Ontario government's Amethyst Award in June 2007. This award recognizes individuals and groups within the Ontario Public Service who have made outstanding contributions in client service, innovation, valuing people and professional achievement.

University of Ottawa Certificate of Appreciation 2006: For collaboration in support of literacy and numeracy research to the Faculty of Education.

The Fred L. Bartlett Memorial Award 2005: Presented by the Ontario Public School Board's Association for outstanding contribution to education throughout Ontario.

The RCM Lifetime Achievement Award 2005: This award celebrates the contribution of an educator who has dedicated his or her life's work to the arts and education and embodies the spirit of Learning Through the Arts.
The Royal Conservatory of Music
Learning Through the Arts

The Order of Ontario 2004: To recognize and honour those who have enriched the lives of others by attaining the highest standards of excellence and achievement in their respective fields.
Government of Ontario

Harry Jerome Award 2002: For excellence in education.
Black Business and Professional Association

Women of Distinction Award 2001: The education award for outstanding contribution to education.
YWCA of Greater Toronto

In Celebration of Women Award 2001: A community-based award for outstanding contribution to education.
Aurora, Ontario

Black History Makers Award 2001: In recognition of excellent service and for being an outstanding, positive role model for the community, in particular, those of Black and Caribbean heritage.
United Achievers Club
Brampton, Ontario

Appreciation Award 2000: For commitment to making the community a better place in which to live and for dedication to the town and the region.
Whitchurch / Stouffville Community

Woman of the Year 2000: For outstanding accomplishments to date and the noble example set for peers and the entire community.
American Biographical Institute and the Board of International Research
U.S.A.

African Canadian Achievement Award 1999: For exemplary contributions of African Canadians to their community and the wider Canadian society.

Certificate of Appreciation 1999: In recognition of outstanding contribution to education and youth of African heritage
Milliken African Caribbean Canadian Upliftment Program

Applause Recognition 1998: For significant contribution to public education in York Region.
York Region District School Board

Founders Award 1997: As a gesture of public recognition for contributions made to P.A.C.E. Canada during the decade 1987-97.
Women for P.A.C.E. Canada
Placed on an Honour Roll

Antiracism and Ethnocultural Equity Award 1997: In recognition of outstanding contribution to antiracist education.
Certificate of Appreciation
York Region Board of Education

Special Citation 1996: In recognition of outstanding contribution to education.
Munro and Dickenson Trust

Appreciation Award 1995: In recognition of outstanding leadership, service and significant contribution to the Ron Edmonds Summer Academy.
Charles D. Moody Institute

Distinguished Educator Award 1995: In recognition of individuals who have made a specific and noteworthy contribution to education within the Province of Ontario or Canada.
The Ontario Institute for Studies in Education

Outstanding Educator of the Year 1995: In acknowledgement of distinguished service to education and in appreciation of leadership in relating the aims, purposes, and objectives of Phi Delta Kappa to public education.
Phi Delta Kappa

Pacesetter Award 1995: In appreciation of special contribution and commitment to the advancement of early childhood education in Canada and Jamaica.
Women for P.A.C.E. Canada

Appreciation Award 1995: In recognition of outstanding leadership, service, and significant contribution to education, equity and the improvement of the African-Canadian community.
Canadian Alliance of Black School Educators

The Morgan D. Parmenter Memorial Award 1992: In recognition of outstanding contribution to Guidance and Counselling in Ontario.
Ontario School Counsellors' Association

International Education Award 1991: In recognition of outstanding contribution to International Education.
Church Teachers' College, Jamaica

International Peace Scholarship 1974-75: For post-graduate studies in education.
P.E.O. Scholarship Foundation

ABOUT THE AUTHOR

Roderick Benns is a Canadian nationalist and is the author of several books, including *Basic Income: How a Canadian Movement Could Change the World* and *The Legends of Lake on the Mountain: An Early Adventure of John A. Macdonald.* He is the founder of Fireside Publishing House, which has captured national media attention for its efforts to increase Canadian historical literacy. He is also the publisher of *The Precarious Work Chronicle* found at precariouswork.com, an emerging news site focused on challenges to Canada's employment and social policy landscape. Roderick spent nine years as senior writer for the Ontario Ministry of Education's Literacy and Numeracy Secretariat and Student Achievement Division. An award-winning author and journalist, he has interviewed former prime ministers of Canada, ministers, and senators, and has written for *The Globe and Mail, Toronto Star,* and *National Post.* Roderick is a sought-after speaker about Canada's history and its leaders, as well as on Basic Income policy. Learn more at www.roderickbenns.net

Printed in Canada